Boat
BASTARD

Boat BASTARD

Deborah van Rooyen

A LOVE/HATE MEMOIR

ReganBooks
An Imprint of HarperCollinsPublishers

Grateful acknowledgment is made for the following:
Artwork on pages v, vii, 2, 6, 68, 162, 184, 192, 248, 254, 255, 258
courtesy of Deborah van Rooyen.
Drawings on pages 26, 112, 253, 259 courtesy of Kierie van Rooyen.
Sheet music on page 140 by permission of the Keepers and Governors
of Harrow School.
Painting on page 226 by Gale Antokal, courtesy of the Couturier Gallery,
Los Angeles.

In the interest of privacy, some of the names, geographical details,
and features of individuals in this book have been changed.

HarperCollins books may be purchased for educational,
business, or sales promotional use.
For information please write: Special Markets Department,
HarperCollins Publishers Inc., 10 East 53rd Street,
New York, NY 10022.

FIRST EDITION

Printed on acid-free paper

Library of Congress Cataloging-in-Publication Data

Van Rooyen, Deborah.
    Boat bastard : a love/hate memoir / Deborah van Rooyen.—1st ed.
    p. cm.
    ISBN 0-06-009354-4 (acid-free paper)
    1. Boats and boating—Fiction.   2. Massachusetts—Fiction.   I. Title.
PS3622.A616 B6 2002
813'.6—dc21   2002021266

02   03   04   05   06   DC/RRD   10   9   8   7   6   5   4   3   2   1

To *Morning Watch,* the Other Woman

. . . and especially for Kierie van Rooyen,

because you loved him, too.

PROLOGUE

REVENGE

The black cloth voodoo doll doesn't even have a prick left. It's a simple form no larger than the size of my hand: small head, stubby arms, short torso, cookie-cutter-shaped legs the color of a blackened gingerbread man kept too long in the oven. A small rip in the inseam where the male organ had been stitched now exposes loose white rag stuffing and ratty newspaper scraps.

But what would you expect? The doll's been through hell over the past ten years.

The voodoo doll was a present from a Haitian piano-mover friend who searched the entire island to find just the right magic to help me through the winter of my first serious breakup with the Captain. I know it's authentic because it works. Why shouldn't it? All the fine points are there: one angry woman, one angry, hurt woman, one box of straight pins, one anatomically correct male voodoo doll.

Two years later, long after that first powerful stab, after the Captain and I kiss and make up, he tells me, he confesses, his in-between girlfriend always had a headache when it came right down to close contact.

I told you it works.

THE END

ESCAPE

CHESAPEAKE BAY

It takes a lot of emotional energy to remember all the details and present them unfairly enough so I come out looking the victim and he the victimizer. It's true because I allow it. Until the last bell, that is, when I jump ship, in the middle of Chesapeake Bay, in the middle of the gala Offshore Yacht Club Sailing Cruise, in the middle of a Papagallo-pink-and-green delegation, in the middle of a southern heat wave, in the middle of a Jewish joke. This is the exact moment in the wave of events when I have enough of the blue blazer tyranny, pack up my duffel bag with the few items of clothing I am allotted to keep stowed in the portside locker of his sailing sloop, trip over the mooring lines on my leap from the deck onto the dock pilings, and hitchhike two hours to the Baltimore airport. I'd like to lie and say I row ashore, then hitchhike to the airport. It's more dramatic. But I don't have to; we are tied up at the town marina, our last morning in civilization before sailing out to the Potomac Islands with a flotilla of retired boat couples who have turned cockpit sitting and bourbon drinking into an un-refined art.

Which brings me to this present evening.

I am lying at home in my own bed, my favorite spot in the entire universe, scribbling furious notes into a wiro-bound, not-so-blank-anymore book. I am trying to muster the verbal credibility to describe a situation so mean, so desperate, you can actually feel my pain—feel the yewing and yawing of the boat I escape from, feel the imprisonment of the sleeping-bunk eighths I stake out as my quarter of the forepeak, feel the breathless claustrophobia, the head door of the toilet locker back-slammed against the inner bed berth; my legs trapped motionless into the narrow V-shape conforming to the angle of the bow of the ship.

Inside the forepeak cabin, my head is propped against the aft wall on two soggy synthetic pillows smelling slightly of mildew. The rest of me is crammed on top of a cranberry-colored lumpy cotton-polyester quilt. The quilt acts as padding to smooth out the uncomfortable jumble of mattress cushions jigsawed beneath my body. The comforter looks bet-ter than it feels; the stiff-ridged cushion seams bite through the quilt into my skin like the Princess and the Pea.

I am motionless because everything else is moving. Each time I make a quick, careless movement reaching left above my shoulder to zip open the mesh netting on the shelf that holds my stash of pill bottles, drinking water, books, I hit my head against the teak side rail.

And the heat.

The white Turkish-taffy-colored sides of the boat sweat like a Southern policeman. Everything is sweating. Even the pages of the book I am reading are damp, perspiring in the humidity. Two portholes, starboard and portside, are screwed shut to keep the sea out and the sweat in. The forepeak hatch is raised up one short inch for a gasp of air above the perfectly aligned screen cover, smartly fitted in place with brass slide locks. The varnish on the teak frame is as shiny as my face.

This is how it is. Even though I am home in bed in Boston, I am still rocking on the boat's berth in the Chesapeake, body immobilized for hours on end, hours and hours, reading *Moby-Dick,* or *The Perfect Storm,* or some other gritty seafaring adventure, all the while feeling as if I am the paralyzed Superman, a living head without the use of my body, locked in solitary confinement.

Why?

Put yourself in my bare feet.

I stay up in the forepeak because it's safer than getting in the way of the Captain. He's already been up since first watch graphing the complicated numbers on the navigational chart with pencil and compass marking headings, buoys, shoals, bells, safe harbors, and reading about the evening's anchorage in preparation for the next eight hours of passage. In his heart he is an Eagle Scout and is always earning merit badges for survival skills. He likes it that I sleep late in the morning. He is free to think only of his boat and her needs and although she can groan, she can't bitch.

Eventually, I have to make an appearance. Mostly because I

have to make use of the bathroom, which at sea is called the *head,* the smell of coffee is too seductive to ignore forever, and the guilt for not lending a hand to weigh anchor rests uneasily on my conscience.

This is what it means to pitch and sway my way topsides:

First I maneuver my legs over the bunk edge and slide my feet down to the floor, not without deflowering myself on the bridge of the V-berth frame. I manage to pinch my upper arm skin on the head door as I move inside to use the facilities and brush my teeth, catching my bare feet on the slightly raised floorboard stall nails. If I'm very lucky, with the head door hooked behind me, I pass by the corner edge of the captain's table in the center salon without incident. Still, somehow I manage to hit the dangling kerosene night lamp, or lurch into the stove knobs on the galley oven when I lean over to pour a cup of coffee for the Captain.

And I'm not up on deck yet.

The low hatch cover planking still waits to smack me in the forehead. If the hatch cover doesn't get me, the steel armature raising the Loran computer screen does, just as I hoist myself up into the cockpit. I enter the Captain's watch splashing a hot cup of coffee upwind as the sloop cuts across the wake of a passing motorboat.

"Good morning," he calls over the noise of the engine in a voice cheerful and hardy.

I squint at him through the glare of the sun. He is a handsome, strapping sea-captain type of man who you wouldn't guess is soon to turn sixty. He stands large with sturdy legs splayed apart at the helm, thick capable hands guiding the cockpit wheel, Polartec jacket halfway zipped, gray-and-white beard shiny with beads of sea spray, salt-and-pepper hair flying back in the wind.

I melt.

His brown eyes wink hello, and he leans forward over the compass cover for a quick kiss, then restlessly moves back to scan the sea, the depth sounder, the sails, the chart, the knot meter, the engine revs, the Loran, the GPS, the chart again. He is happy out in the elements. The wind is refreshing when we are cruising at a clip. Even cold. I move onto the cockpit cushions in direct line with the sun. I reach for his warm hand, give it a tug hello, and pass him the half-filled coffee mug. This is the best time of the morning. We are under way and at peace.

The black-and-blue marks will only surface later.

CLAUSTROPHOBIA

THE BOAT YARD, CAPE COD

The Captain is the skipper of a blue-hulled, teak-decked, elegant-lined, thirty-six-foot fiberglass, van Leuwenhoek–designed sailing sloop with a Choy Lee gold-inlaid insignia identifiable by a pattern of dragon tails on the bowsprit. Some other avid adventurer hauls this sailboat from its Hong Kong shipyard over to Prigmore's Boat Yard down the Cape in the early 1970s, probably by container ship. I have no idea of its initial history. I only know that title, registration, and money exchange hands at a restaurant on the exit by Routes 1 and 128 in Massachusetts, and the broker walks away happy.

I soon learn a *sloop* is not a *yawl* is not a *ketch* is not a *schooner*. But it is a *yacht*.

Don't ask me to elaborate, because I don't know what the

exact differences are between sailboats except that the types have something to do with the mast and the mainsail and where the masts and mainsails are positioned in relation to the cockpit and bow. The Captain knows every rig, the name and origin of every sail, and that's enough for me. He tells me the sailboat is a sloop, and I believe him.

This much I do know:

The Captain's sailboat is a graceful, single-mast vessel, puffed up with one enormous proud white mainsail. When the wind fills the main and side sails, the boat skips forward across the waves like a fashionable woman waving her white hand-kerchief for a taxi on the Champs Élysées in Paris. It is truly an elegant sight.

But then it depends on your point of view.

With the hot noon sun beating behind the mainsail, the rise of the silhouetted wooden toe rails fastened on the sides of the short cabin roof can also look like a fist of brass knuckles. And carry as much punch if you are unlucky enough to lurch into their territory.

The swell of the half-moon-shaped *dodger,* a white canvas awning with two clear plastic zip-open windows, humps the horizon line. Equivalent in function to a car windshield, the dodger sits spread-eagle across the hatch, and acts as a great barrier reef separating the bracing sea spray from the shocked expression of the Captain in the cockpit after a wave rolls higher than the dodger and splashes his face with the force of an indignant woman giving a rude man one quick unexpected slap. *Here, take that.* And he does.

The cockpit is a four-man indentation of sitting cushions aft of the cabin on deck. The area is the heart of the sailboat be-cause it houses the wheel, the *helm,* and the chest-height compass whose 360 degrèes loll about beneath a shiny chrome cover called the *binnacle*. Three inches up from the floorboards and just underfoot juts the stub of the emergency tiller wrapped like an amputated limb in a piece of leather. The tiller's day job is to catch bare toes for a living.

The navigation wheel is big, or I am not big enough to see over it. In order to see where I'm steering, I need to stand up on the cockpit seat, legs spread left and right on the cushions for balance, lean forward, and hold on to the wheel with both hands. This way I can stretch to look over the dodger and eye the rolling sea in between the flapping mainsail and jib that shade the sea like a shark's fin while the Captain grabs a nap below. This is a difficult and solitary position to be in for hours.

But I am never really alone at the helm.

The *dinghy,* the small escape rowboat, trails behind our sloop like a punished child in exile. Doggedly determined to catch up, the dinghy is held astern by a ten-foot length of rope. Essential for survival at sea, the dinghy is also useful for carrying smoldering plastic garbage bags downwind, a set of oars, lifesaving gear, and sometimes my six-year-old daughter tethered in a life jacket playing with her Barbie dolls when the seas are calm and she is restless. As the dinghy hits each wake, her laughter smacks above the splashes in delight until the laugh turns into a whine and she wants to come on board the mother ship again.

I do know the sloop is thirty-six feet of narrow space from bow to stern—like six Captains lying head to toe. And on a yacht, size is definitely an issue. Thirty-six feet means wishing you could condense every item of gear into a neat little floppy disk with a Stuffit Deluxe software program. This includes compressing pots, dishes, clothes, books, towels, quilts, pillows, buckets, toolboxes, radio batteries, pumps, fuel, life jackets, and all the other urgent equipment until you need it, which you always do eventually.

Down below, the only stuffit program available is the manual kind. This requires squashing clothes into one narrow hanging locker already bulging with his dozen Eddie Bauer long-sleeve cotton shirts, a Savile Row blue blazer with brass buttons, a lightweight yellow slicker, a few hangers weighted down by his cotton pants, and the Captain's four pairs of equally weather-beaten Timberland boat shoes. Oh yes, and two very wrinkled black Flax summer dresses I beg permission to hang up in case we ever need to eat ashore in style.

There is one wet locker behind the ice chest for hanging the foul-weather gear. Everything else is stowed under the salon seats or on the shelves behind the stove, above the ice chest, in the head behind the sink, and under the pilot's berth in oversize drawers that pull out only with an enormous tug and are packed with charts, an autopilot, duct tape, tools, and extras of every possible engine part that could need replacing if we are to sail offshore and have no access to a ship's chandlery. There is one secret spot under the dining bench cushions for the big guns: fifths of gin, bottles of bourbon, Meyer's dark rum, a case of tonic water, a liter of malt whiskey, two bottles of Scotch, a gallon of Stoli, extra flasks of Cointreau, and a few bottles of select California wines. We are regularly prepared for Best Buddy, the Captain's old prep-school roommate and present-tense retirement sailing partner.

When I bring my gear on board, it's always a tug of war between cramming my three T-shirts, two sarongs, and a few pair of mismatched underwear into plastic baggies and then finding one foot of free space to stow them within reach. I have two choices: I can force them in between the mountains of extra quilts and jumbo garbage bags swollen with guest bath towels and unused sails on my side of the cabin shelf, or stash them into the impossible-to-open drawers deep under the sleeping-berth cushions, which means never getting to them at all.

In short, there is no room for me on board.

It takes thirteen years, but I eventually get the message.

ENGINE TROUBLE

SOMEWHERE AT SEA

We are skimming over the waves toward the port of choice for the night.

I am having a late lunch of Pepperidge Farm Mint Milano cookies up on deck.

He prefers something cooler and liquidlike.

This is where I can make a difference on the boat.

I can skip down below and bring up an O'Doul's nonalcoholic beer while he's stuck at the wheel when the sun is at its fiercest. It is one task I can never say no to, because he'd sooner keel over from dehydration than admit that his outflow is a condensed yellow.

So down I go, pulling open the heavy door to the ice chest, and immediately smash my thumb on the jammed brass locker hardware. I swear, suck the skin, then dive my raw fingertips over ice blocks as sharp-edged as broken glass. I am digging down deep into the chest to reach the coldest bottles crammed tightly into a space no bigger than a breadbox. I reach to pull up the frosty winner. All the dozens of remaining chilled bottles, all the tiers of food stacked in plastic shelves, all shift and tumble back to fill the void, skinning the knuckles of my hand, which is still gripping the chosen drink like an Olympic torch.

Is it worth a reward of a bite-size frozen Snickers?

But that's another excavation.

The Snickers bars are glazed onto the skin of the aluminum ice tray, which can only make ice when the engine is running. If the engine is running, it means we are motoring. We are only motoring when there is no wind, or no wind coming in the right direction, or the wind is behind us, or the wind is on our nose. Or we are motoring when we are heading south down the narrow Intracoastal Waterway, charting our progress over speed canal bumps or holding steady waiting for the bridge master to stop car traffic and open the drawbridge so we can pass through into the next channel. Or when we are cruising north in the cold-water inlets of rugged Maine, negotiating our way through the land mines of lobster traps. Then the engine is on, which means it is usually incredibly noisy, a headachy kind of noise droning out the sound of gulls and egrets and the splash of porpoises or seals diving alongside the boat. The constant grinding whir of pistons spewing diesel fumes creates a mechanical cacophony so loud you can't even hear the Captain shouting orders.

But I make my delivery, passing him the O'Doul's along with a couple of mini Snickers treats.

When the Captain sees the blood on my knuckles, he shakes his head and says, *"You move too fast,"* and worries I'll stain the cockpit cushions.

I now have to go back down below to find the box of Band-Aids.

But back to the engine.

The engine does two good things in terms of comfort: it makes ice (that's for his comfort in the drinks at sunset), and it makes hot water (this is mine)—allowing for a one-minute shower squeezed inside the head locker, which is even smaller than the icebox.

A hot shower is pure luxury if you like to go to bed with sweet-smelling armpits and can tolerate soapy hair, because the water trickles out in the middle of the rinse cycle. Or you can be like the boys, stick it out with brown bum smear marks and streak the sheets.

SCENE: *Salon.* TIME: *21:30.* ANCHORAGE: *Vineyard Haven, Vinyl Haven, Camden Harbor, Gloucester Bay, St. George's Island, Redbrook Harbor, Seal Point, Isle of Shoals*

The Captain is sprawled out on the bunk opposite the galley table. Well, not exactly sprawled, because of the narrowness of the pilot's berth, but comfortably stretched; one hand propping up his raw-burned, shining dome of a head that's still got a few tufts of hair left on top, the other tucked into the waistband of his pants, inching toward the center of his existence. I sit at the bottom of the bunk, his feet resting on my lap. Rugby-player legs in gray cotton sailing pants exposing tanned ropy-veined ankles end in bare feet and gnarled, waterlogged toes. Toughened toenails, almost prehistoric in mutation, nudge my hand for a foot massage, but I pass.

Next to his prone head, two inches to his right on the chart table, a snifter glass of Cointreau is almost ready for another refill. Midsentence I catch a snore, or a Hastings School–sized boy's fart accompanied by a naughty grin, a *you just have to love me, don't you,* and then a half smile, more charming than pleading *could you just scratch the top of my head, please. Oh, yes, that's it, a little to the left. Can you feel a bump? Am I broken? Purr. Purr.*

Our kindest moments are like the after-dinner warmth of the orange liqueur radiating from toe to scalp. Big paws reach out for a refill. A quick wink, the tiny light of the kerosene lamp dimmed for atmosphere or thrift. Whichever way you look at it, all is peaceful. Tender.

There will be enough hot water.

In the slice of space between the table and the berth, I extricate my lap from his feet, slide lengthwise against him, untie the drawstring of my traffic-light-yellow men's flannel pajama bottoms, and let them drop. His eyebrows rise an inch in interest. I find his lips tasting of orange liqueur mixed with rum. As I press myself into the crook of his broad shoulders, my hands move to unbutton his shirt and continue down with the pant's zipper, dragging the cotton trousers down the thighs and extricating them from the tangle at his feet. I toss his pants toward the seven seas.

My pajama top goes next. Then his T-shirt.

"Come with me," I tease.

Shivering in the night air, I take him by the hand and squeeze us together into the minuscule teak-paneled head. He is woozy and agreeable.

I sit him skin pink on top of the toilet seat, turn the water nozzle to mix hot with cold, fill the sink, washcloth warming in the suds. Water on, I splash both our bodies from head down. Water off, washcloth scrubbing forehead, scalp, beard, ears, neck, and beyond, getting all the parts right down to the toes. Water on. Splash. Water off. Coaxing like mother with child, I turn him around, pressing my chilled body into the warmth of his strong back, now a clean soapy smell, slip the soapy cloth between his thighs, make a detour, then head down, down to his feet.

We laugh together like little kids caught playing doctor.

Again the shower hose, hot-water luxury, two splashes for each of us. Water off. A capful of shampoo dabbed into the palm of my hand, massaging what is left of his straight gray-white hair, his captain's beard. Then my own hair, sudsing.

A fast thirty-second rinse follows. The porthole glass steams, the mirror fogs, the runoff water sloshes over the Formica sink countertop, down the paneling into the basin below the floorboards. We stand joined on the rubber-gripped mat, our two clean bodies drip-drying. Our damp towels rest a little longer than an arm's reach away outside the door.

"I'll get them," he volunteers. "Don't move."

Handing me my orange towel, he turns away and dries himself with his own gray color-coded terry cloth, shuddering slightly like a wet dog. I can see he is pleased although he is wearing a *don't tell Best Buddy* abashed look.

He smells great. If I can get the toothbrush armed and ready, the job might almost be complete before the final leap up under the forepeak quilts.

The end of the night is the best part of the day.

Intimate, cocooned in the V-berth, lamps lit, toes touching, we open our separate books to read together. We are lucky. There are no storms this night, just a slight sea breeze. The night is quiet, the loll of the sea rolls the boat and rocks us gently. Topsides, the halyard slaps rhythmically. On deck, the wood boards groan like the winding mechanism of an old Viennese music box.

He is exhausted. He doesn't make it to the next page. The snore comes quickly, seconds after his big hand reaches to pull me closer. I want to make love. We have been together for more than a decade of years. This is the man I wait for. I always wait. I nuzzle him awake with a kiss on his neck. He smiles contentedly in the dark.

"Snuggle in," he says.

We feel the sweetness of our spanking-clean skin against each other. The warmth spreads.

"Oh my God," he says, "I forgot to take my pills!"

We giggle. We are getting old. It's ridiculous but funny. I volunteer to fetch them.

"Would you?" he asks like a little boy. "Do you mind?"

I twist out to lower myself down from the berth and smack my head on the overhang.

"Move slowly," he reminds me.

The floorboards are chilly and damp. I unlatch the door to the head, slide open the swollen slatted cabinet door, pull out his ditty bag, and retrieve the medicine. The drinking water is more complicated, involving a trip to the ice chest. I stand on tippy toes, hands dip into the frozen depths of beer and Coke cans until I reach the gallon of springwater. Take everything out. Put everything back. I pull out a plastic drinking glass from a tight regimental row above the ice chest. The remaining glasses list back into position.

The Captain is a big man. I am much smaller, shorter, softer. Together our bulk eats up the boat's free space. He is careful. I, impulsive. So it is best when one of us stays still while the other moves around.

I carry the water glass and two white pills carefully back to bed. He is already deep in sleep.

THE TOP DRAWER

Sometimes after I reread these pages I am amazed at how accurately I describe the situation. Perhaps it's the pen I write with. This one is miserable, a skinny blue Bic fine point with a gold Hotel Forum, Kraków logo stamped up the side. *Kraków, Poland*. The memory of the forbidding country, city, Jewish Holocaust theme park I visit two weeks ago with my surviving Israeli cousins makes me want to drop it quickly. *Good idea*. Out with this pen. I can't think in Bic Fine Point, especially in Kraków Bic Fine Point. And I can't think about Poland right now. I can't think about the inky tattoo on my uncle's forearm. I can't think about the family farmhouse where first they shot the dog, then my grandparents. Let me save that journey for later.

My Sharpie rescues the night.

I always keep a secret stockpile of black felt-tip pens in the top drawer of my dresser tucked beneath a plastic bag of expired passports, a twice-washed 1972 Israeli Army identity card inside a faded blue *teudat zeheut,* one late-sixties' Dutch-issued international driver's license, three former university and graduate-school passes, and a stack of blue plastic health center/hospital ID cards from lives' past. The Haitian voodoo doll lies airlessly in another Ziploc bag, tangled in red thread, odd lots of sewing needles, a thimble. I think twice. The deed is done. No need to crank up the meter. Not even a short ping. I remind myself I do have the power. It's really the only thing I do have.

In that top drawer I still stash old letters, or, more accurately, brief angry communications sent by the Captain after every major fight. His letterhead stationery is marked with a dyad of bold, identifying logos designed by me—one for the Cape house, one for the boat. I fashion the very weapons which joust me in the heart. Do I quote them? Frankly I don't feel like opening the envelopes, rereading the words that hurt the first time, the second time, the third time. Maybe later, when the self-inflicted pain goes too far, I'll drag out the evidence.

But not yet. *Maybe never.*

But were we on the boat? Soaping down? Showering? Wasting water? Is that where I left us?

Hold that memory for another chapter or two, it has some sweetness I wish to keep current. It's late, and dragging up the rancor at this hour just keeps me up and angry the rest of the night.

THE BEGINNING

TAKE ONE

THE STUDIO

I don't know if I explain myself adequately: the man that I love is not the man that I love sailing.

When I first meet the Captain, he is not a captain. He is a hot advertising film director. His reputation for shooting the best sixty-second commercial spots runs after him not only in Boston but also up and down the East Coast. He is very talented, very successful. He directs a busy studio with scads of adoring assistants, big-name agencies, bigger-named clients. He makes a lot of money. Later I find out it's a good thing, because he spends a lot of money supporting two ex-wives, two divorce lawyers, a strike-it-rich stockbroker, and a pricey Cape Cod yacht marina. He has everybody eating out of the palm of his wallet. He never stops moving. He works twenty-four-hour days six days a week for thirty years. Then it's five days a week. Then once he gets this retirement notion, only whenever he's booked a year in advance for a month at a time.

In the beginning of his career, he fathers two sets of twins, all boys, then one more son, one year immediately after another, who see about as much of him as does his first wife, which is much less than his clients. He is so exhausted he naps when the traffic light turns red. He is born competitive, relentless. He is fiercely independent yet demands a lot of attention. Because he is charming, he gets it. He propels himself with enormous determination into the center of the sixty-second-spot-commercial world despite an Ivy League degree in economics he uses for supply-and-demand billing and how to get paid in less than sixty days.

He needs to be important without anyone knowing who his father is (a foreign diplomat), the pedigree of his mother (a Southern debutante), where he went to school (an upper-class English public school), where he grew up (Washington, D.C., the French Belgian Congo, London, Berlin).

But that's a pinch of the whole story.

I first hire him for a commercial shoot I'm art-directing with a big budget that can support his ego, and am annoyed when he throws all his attention to my junior assistant, who happens to be a male. He doesn't look at me, acknowledge me, consult with me, even though I'm buying. By the end of the shoot, he tells my male assistant he'll call him sometime for lunch. I see him take out my assistant within the week, with a brief nod to me as we pass in the reception area of the agency. I always wonder why he is barking up the wrong tree. I shrug my shoulders and buy my own lunch at the take-out deli on the corner. But I'm hurt.

Six months go by.

I am on another location shoot in Tucson, Arizona, with a different crew. At the end of the long workday, a Navajo stunt-man hands me a brightly feathered kachina doll and tells me it's a powerful Native American symbol for fertility.

"Touch the doll and soon there'll be a lover," he predicts.

Startled, I drop the doll from my hands into my lap, then as quickly toss the hot-potato fertility kachina back to the stuntman.

"No thanks." I blush.

The next day I fly back to my steady life as a single mother.

And to a phone call.

The Captain is on the line.

"My assistant's out today," I tell him when the receptionist buzzes him through to me, I think by mistake.

"How about lunch?" he invites with great charm, ignoring my brush-off.

"Busy," I say.

And I am. I have a client meeting at noon.

"How about dinner?"

"Tonight?" I am surprised.

"Yes."

"Sorry, I can't," I answer. And I really can't. "I have to be somewhere at eight."

"I'll buy you a drink at seven. Tell me where."

He is persuasive, persistent, polite. I am thinking he is thinking I have some imminent work project for him. But I don't. I feel guilty for wasting his time. What I do have is a standing Tuesday-evening therapy appointment to discuss the hardships of single parenting. I don't tell him this, yet. I'm also wondering what he's not telling me.

"Okay." I relent. "Just for a quick drink. How about the Rover Café?"

"See you," he says. "Gotta run."

Click. The conversation is over.

But I can hear him smiling.

BLIND DATES

I know a woman art director who is so tough, her nickname is Slugger. She goes on a blind date with a never-even-married-once film director who spends the entire evening talking on and on about himself. Throughout dinner, even after dessert (which she doesn't order), he never once asks her anything about who she is, about her dreams, her life.

When the waiter brings the check, he asks her to go dutch.

The woman art director faxes him an invoice the next day for three hours of consultation services plus travel time. The film director is very angry and insulted. He calls her office and, when she won't take his call, starts screaming at the receptionist.

I don't think he ever gets the point.

THE FIRST DRINK

THE ROVER CAFÉ

He is waiting at a small table, nursing the ice in a sophisticated-looking cocktail I don't recognize because Jews don't drink. We are the only two in the restaurant lounge. Everyone else is inside the dining room eating dinner.

I don't mind. I only have time for appetizers.

(The dialogue goes something like this:)

- We talk work.
- We move on.
- I listen to the whole story of his recent separation from Wife #2.
- He listens to the whole story of my daughter's kid-

napping by my ex-husband and her traumatic front-page recovery in South Africa.

- He seems to care, and tells me, "I'm pretty sensitive for a guy."
- I check my wristwatch and tell him, "I've got to go."
- Before I leave, I lean over and give him one impulsive kiss on the vulnerable back of his neck as a thank-you for paying attention.
- I surprise myself.
- I surprise him.

He asks, as I am running out the door:
"What are you doing next Tuesday night?"

ORIGINAL SIN

When the Captain and I first connect, I am already working a more-than-full-time, high-stress job as the design director for a sizable advertising agency. I travel to our other twenty-two offices a lot, flying in, flying out, always racing, always making arrangements, always barely making the on-the-dot-or-else day-care pickups for my preschool daughter by 6 P.M. I am paid more than most single mothers, but a lot less than most men in the same field. At the time I don't know my true value and think I need only to keep pace with inflation.

Eventually, I buy a hundred-year-old, crooked, three-story, almost-in-Boston row house with a kitchen in the basement for a lot more money than it is worth. I make the down payment myself. I get the mortgage myself. I support my only daughter myself. The house inspector says the house is a can of worms. But the location is perfect, because the school district is perfect. When we move in, my young daughter is afraid to sleep in her new bedroom. She thinks worms are squiggling behind the walls, in her closet, downstairs under the kitchen cabinets. But I am optimistic. I renovate and paint every free weekend for the next ten years.

Day-to-day it's the regular routine:

I take the garbage out on Tuesday nights, along with the recycling bins of sorted glass and paper cartons. I keep up with the piles of daily laundry in a mini portable washing machine I wheel up to hook into the kitchen faucet. I open 9-Lives cans of fishy-smelling tuna to feed two pushy cats with one hand while pouring bowls of Cheerios for my starving daughter with the other. The cereal is only to hold her until I run to the supermarket at rush hour to get a gallon of milk and three-for-a-dollar boxes of macaroni and cheese because we've run out of everything.

I clean the house on Saturday mornings with a temperamental, broken-wheeled vacuum cleaner with a too-short cord. I get temperamental right back. When I'm not on a short fuse, I make big Friday-night dinners with roast chicken and salad and entertain friends who agree to bring dessert. I only mention this because I don't have the energy to talk about the twenty-four-hour-a-day mothering details or get into the daily work worries that keep me lying awake at night.

Later, after the Captain and I become an item and we intersect our lives, it's off to his new/old house down the Cape on weekends. Pet-care arrangements are always being made because he says *no* to bringing the cats. This becomes a major issue once I add a small, white, fluffy, fur-shedding, devoted

Eskimo dog who can't live without me to the already crowded dynamic. The Captain says absolutely *no* to her and refuses to budge. He claims her paws will scratch the house's slick varnish protecting the boat-shiny, pristine pine-and-ash floors.

Leaving the dog behind in the city on weekends hurts me. I love my dog and the feeling is beyond mutual. The dog even loves the Captain. And she's very fussy. I think she leaps into his arms when he comes in the door to my house because he's white and fluffy, too. When I catch him blissfully dozing with her tucked under the crook of his shoulder on my bed one night after I pop unexpectedly out of the bath to grab a towel, he denies everything.

But when we're down the Cape, we are on his territory and I try to understand his position. His position is firm.

"No dogs."

The consideration for the floors also means taking our shoes off the second my bouncing daughter and I cross the threshold. On and off, off and on, every time we go in and out.

And we are coming and going more than we are staying.

I am always running, packing, unpacking, filling the gas tank, refilling the gas tank, fighting the weekend traffic over the bridge, fighting the weekend traffic back, and those are the weekends when there are no soccer games, swim-team meets, birthday parties, gymnastics, Sunday school. When that's the case, we head to the Cape late on Saturday afternoons.

When I call out of breath to tell him I'm running behind, he always answers, *"No pressure."*

He is very patient about my daughter. He understands. He has five sons from his first wife. And a stepson from his second. While they are growing up he is very busy working and sailing. Now that they are grown up, he is still very busy working and sailing. But he is always available by phone. But boys are not girls.

My daughter is much less patient about him.

Over the spread of years, he is not really in. And he is not really out.

My daughter gets it right the very first night I finally let him sleep over on the couch in the living room. She is only three and a half, but already she knows how to count. The arithmetic is simple: The two-bedroom house doesn't fit three.

It is 5:30 on a Sunday morning. He is asleep in the living room. My daughter should be asleep in her room. I lie awake in my own bed. I am rarely awake at this hour because it is usually prime sleeping time after hours of tossing and turning. I don't get that far this early morning. My heart is racing.

The night before, he comes over to dinner. After a late-night video movie where we argue over the name of the director and I win, he reaches over to kiss me. The romantic move takes me completely by surprise. Of course I want him to kiss me. He is the most attractive and magnetic man I have encountered in years. He also seems enormously sensitive, tender, even interested in me. I like the fact that he is twelve years older than I am. He seems sophisticated, smart, well traveled, a great storyteller. We have a lot of globe-trotting in common. We have our successful, high-profile careers in common. We have our broken marriages in common. We have our broken children, our broken hearts in common. I think maybe he's even a good listener for a guy. After I share a few painful secrets, he tells me I am a wounded bird. I agree and lift my broken wing. That's when his discovery of what's under my loose painter shirt comes up.

"You have breasts!" he stammers.

His amazement amazes me. Of course I do.

Soon he discovers I also have other things.

Never mind the rest of the details.

Later, much later, he asks to sleep over. I think maybe he has nowhere to go; his second wife has the house; the first wife, the alimony.

So I let him. Sleep over, that is. Just not with me.

By the wee hours of the morning, however, I weaken. My pounding heart yanks me out of my bed and pulls me toward the living room. I creep in next to his warm body and there is no turning back. The sofa mattress is flipped out on the rug, floor level.

He moves over to make room for me. It's wonderful, for a brief minute.

We are not alone.

My little daughter is blinking down at us, twirling her un-combed curls into knots of bull's-eyes with a fist of fingers, her right thumb stuck stubbornly in her mouth.

"*What's he doing here?*" she wants to know.

He stays silent. He might be on the spot, but I am on the stand.

"He's sleeping over," I say.

"Why are you not in your bed, Mommy?"

I feel like I am the guilty party in a letter about divorced women from an Ann Landers advice column. I scramble for an answer but come up, instead, with a quick plan.

It's too early for cartoons, and besides, we're lying right in front of the television set.

"I have an idea," I tell her. "Why don't you go get the big pad of paper and all your crayons and draw a picture?"

She looks at me with suspicion, then suddenly disappears,

her little golden curls leaving an afterglow of defiant disapproval like a quivering halo that has lost its angel.

But she is back lickety-split.

"What should I draw for Sam?" she asks.

"His name is not Sam," I correct her.

"Oh, what should I draw for Peter?"

"His name is not Peter."

She goes through a list of every male name she has ever heard mentioned in the house, on the phone, at the office—from the delivery guy, to the piano tuner, to my boss at work, and ten others in between. Still, she cannot get his name right.

I am sure I must be very red in the face, as if I have a lineup of strange men in my bed every night. In truth, there has been a long, dry season since the divorce and this present morning that I fill rereading old comfortable books or watching videos with happier endings. I never consider there are real-life men available who want to shoulder a thirty-six-year-old single mother carrying expensive baggage she still owes eighteen more years of duty on. Until now.

"Tell me, Mommy, what should I make for Ben?"

"Weren't you going to draw a picture?" I say, ignoring her latest wrong name. My tone is not so sweet.

My child sits herself down by the edge of the mattress and sticks her pajama feet out so they touch the corner of the pillow my head half rests on. She lays the newsprint pad of paper between her legs and starts scribbling with an exaggerated hand.

The Captain is still silent. But now a winning smile flashes across his face. He is trying to let me know he's experienced with this sort of thing. *No big deal. Not to worry.*

"Let's see. What should I draw?"

"Draw anything," I warn in a tone that means business. I can see that any further chance of sleeping is absolutely finished for all three of us.

She is very busy. I hope she will stay busy for another hour. I am not so lucky. I clock her at half a minute.

"Here, Mommy. Here's a picture of *him*."

She holds up the pad, beaming a child's sweet smile. Even I can read her three-and-one-half-year-old giant Crayola marks.

"It's a snake!" she announces.

He looks.

I look.

It certainly is. We all stare at a tabloid-size picture of a big snake that looks exactly like an inflated condom. How does she know how to draw this? I don't believe she even knows the story of Adam and Eve, or has ever heard of Dr. Freud.

But she knows.

Apparently she is gratified by the reaction. She is busy again, hard at work.

"Here." She holds the pad up to my nose.

The page is the same. The snake is still there.

Only now, the snake has hair.

"What's that?" I ask.

"That's you, Mommy!"

She is very proud.

I am horrified.

He is still quiet.

And that's how it really begins.

I don't remember much more of the morning except that I am charmed when he goes around the house screwing knobs onto pot lids, hanging window blinds onto windows, and helping with other Sunday fix-it chores like a real family man.

"I'm really very domestic," he tells me. Then takes off.

Later I realize this basic domestic display is not for my benefit. It is really for Wife #2, to prove he is a decently trained husband type and that she should never have walked out on him.

*

By the way, I can prove this story of the snake. I saved the picture.

What I don't do is pay attention to the message.

BACKGROUND CHECK

Maybe it's time to let you in on a visual secret, that what I look like has no connection whatsoever with tall, slim, leggy women whose eastern-seaboard names are Missy or Buffy or even Katherine with a K. I don't believe I have an ounce of Protestant blood in me.

On the other hand, if you are picturing a short, dark, curly-haired New York intellectual type with Jewish genes wearing T-shirts stamped with political slogans, you're also wrong.

Let's start first with the geography:

Move the New York topography to Boston via Jerusalem. Think art school, advertising agencies, printers, design studios. Think back and forth to Logan Airport. Think last year to Amman, Jordan. Think two years back to Paris. Think thirty years back to ironing shirts in the laundry on a kibbutz. Think of Israeli Army duty in a ten-man outpost on the sandy Sinai desert road to Cairo before the Yom Kippur War. Think of vagabonding through Thailand and Japan to forget about the Sinai Desert. Think of an impulse wedding in Cape Town, South Africa, to forget about turning thirty. Think of a baby girl and a divorce in Boston before turning thirty-two. Think of raising a child and working nonstop at thirty-four.

But don't think of staying put. Not yet. I haven't met my sailor yet.

Now for the physical details:

Whatever you're picturing, only the short is accurate—five feet plus two inches as measured in the doctor's office of any country. Scratch out *intellectual* and mark in *typical art director/designer who wears a lot of black.* Include black leggings, black elastic snapping sandals, black very comfortable Danish clogs, black tencel oversized painter shirts with long tails, black nobby designed arty smocks that cover the bad parts, of which there are many.

Black clothes means straight, Dutch blond hair and that's just about the shiny color streaked on today. I can't remember its original color because it hasn't been original since I turned sixteen. When I am an eighteen-year-old kibbutz volunteer, and then three years as a university student in Israel, my hair runs down past my shoulders, which gets a lot of attention when you're trying to thumb a ride through the Middle East. I finally cut my hair after the blond turns green in an overchlorinated swimming pool at a five-dollar-per-night Bangkok hotel. Since then, the hair can't make it past a short blunt cut without irritating me.

Today almost thirty years later, this same still-lightened hair frames blue-gray eyes with the beginnings of tired lines and a quirky half smile that turns slightly crooked when you see the teeth. I don't actually hate my face. I just don't like the ·age. Especially below the neck. Of course I could stand to lose ten pounds—okay, make that twenty, although I should probably start with a reasonable goal like five, first. Or exercise. A lot. But I don't. Instead, I avoid mirrors.

Like most women, I have a hate/hate relationship with my body. My skin-and-bones older sister, who has frizzy hair she detests, and I try to re-create a better DNA package when we get together; my hair, her thin body, my shoe size, her long legs, my fair skin, her narrow elegant nose. The mouth is a toss-up; she has wide full lips with giant straightened white teeth, but my wry smile and offbeat looks have the ability to light up a room when I'm in a good mood. My sister says I'm cute, and when I am two years old, I probably am. Today, I'm glad she protects me from the truth. I'd do the same for her, too, if it were necessary, but it's not. She still looks great. And she's still thin.

On the other hand, my sister and I can't agree on whose character should dominate our DNA model. The truth is, we're both impossible. She is rigid in frame, dogmatic in politics, and driven by justice and fair play, a workhorse with asthma. I am intolerant but unbiased: I hate all people equally. Especially in crowded restaurants and post office lines. Then I am foot-tappingly impatient. In a blink, I could annihilate a whole movie theater filled with cracking-gum chewers or erase entire continents of nations whose social quirks irritate me with the delete button on the computer. And that's just an introduction. My older sister and I wonder if our younger sister is the most brilliant of the three, the most tolerant, the most relaxed, the least tense, but her meditative nature about almost everything frustrates our relentless determination to always be doing something. Like writing this book.

The point is, any man who buys into us will never be bored, but will often be furious. We're a tough crowd. So how is it we have rarely been without a man in our lives? I think it's because we are good in bed. How do I know? Is that presumptuous to say? It's not an issue of talent. I'm sure it's in the genes. My mother, we three sisters, my now-seventeen-year-old daughter, we like the opposite sex, even if we don't actually respect them. I can still hear my mother's advice: "Girls, if you have to lie back for the rest of your lives, you might as well make up your minds and enjoy it."

I take that as any excuse to be in bed.

Maybe that's why the Captain and I stay together. Because our physical life is good. For him, sex is a nonissue because we have it. Intimate, naughty, nice, romantic, exciting, guiltless. Especially when we're not on the boat, but alone down at his new/old house at the Cape where there's room to maneuver, even to take deep satisfying baths together in the two-person Victorian claw-foot tub he installs in the master bathroom especially for me. The Cape house means to be off watch, off guard, to ignore the telephone, the weather, the time. It means dry sheets, giant Velux skylights that keep the wet weather out, a thermostat to control the heat, a ceiling fan for cool air. Midafternoons mean naps. Midmornings mean coffee in bed. Together. It is the crazy gorilla glue that sticks us together, this sexual chemistry.

That's why the voodoo doll works. He will know, if you should ever ask him about it, exactly what I mean, because when we're not at each other's throats, we're at each other's zippers.

A FEW FACTS

BOSTON AND THE CAPE

1. The Captain and I do not live together.

I buy my own house in Boston. He buys his own house down the Cape. I spend weekends with him there when he's home. He spends weekday nights with me at my house in the city when he's not working late, or shooting on location, or sailing down the coast, or jumping over to France to visit his ailing father, or running off to the West Coast to visit his sons, or watching *Monday Night Football*. We keep our own clothes in our own closets.

2. We often work together.

I am his client. He is my supplier. I hire him when I have the budget. He shoots my big projects and does good work. I art-direct the visuals and push until the final click. He films my ideas and jumps through hoops to get them on film. I often change my mind while we're shooting. He tries to stay loose and sometimes loses it. But only after the clients leave.

3. Money is not an issue in our relationship.

He tells me I make a lot of money for a girl. But he charges more money in a day than I make in two weeks. I tell him he's expensive. He tells me I am the first woman to buy him dinner. I tell him he is the first man to buy me cocktails. When we first meet, he is broke and I am not. Thirteen years later when we break up, I am broke and he is not. Money is not an issue in our relationship. Everything else is.

4. When the Captain talks, everyone listens.

He calls me every night when we're apart. The first year I listen to him talk for hours about his separation and trials with Wife #2 until they finally divorce. I hurt for him. I strategize with him. I wait for him to ask me *how are you?* and mean it. After two years, I finally put the telephone down and tell him to call back when he is interested in me. He tells me I have no manners because I am interrupting and hangs up on me first. I hang up on him when he calls back, and then panic that he'll never call me again.

5. He reminds me of a dangling carrot.

Even though he is always slightly out of reach except under the sheets, I count on him to be there and am angry when he's not. Sometimes he comes through. Sometimes he slips through.

CHANGING THE TABLES

BOSTON (Appetitos, Bertucci's, the Blue Diner, the Border Café, Bo-Shing, East Coast Grill, Hamersley's Bistro, The Harvest, Sorentos, Santarpios):

THE CAPE (The Beehive, the Black Dog Café, Chatham Bars Inn, Chillingsworth, The Crocker House, Marshlands, Sagamore Inn):

Do I have to be fair and tell you everything I haven't?

My meditative younger sister is reading this unfinished manuscript in the next room. She says the book needs more balance. That the Captain will get aggravated if I don't write more about how I am often a complete lunatic. And not only when there is a full moon. She gently suggests I need to tell how difficult I am to get along with, how impossible my demands are. How she thinks the Captain usually puts up with all of my quirks for so many years, well, because he must have loved me.

I know what she is hinting at. She has been the family observer since birth. Nothing passes her eyes without an edit. She thinks the book will be more interesting if I tell the truth.

"And don't forget to mention how nuts you are in a restaurant."

She's right. He's right.

I am a master at trying to control the environment at all costs. In a restaurant this means moving chairs, changing tables, fidgeting in a seat, not listening to anyone else talking without interrupting, because when I'm talking, I'm interested, and when I'm ignored, I get bored.

Even before we get to the table, the Captain tries to give me etiquette pointers:

"Let the maître d' seat us."

I always disagree with his choice. I need the table by the window, the table in the corner, the table under the air conditioner, not the table next to the lunching mothers barricaded behind a crush of Aprica strollers and shrieking toddlers, or the table shoved up against the blond model with her breasts spilling out of her red slit of a dress and her tongue-hanging-out date.

If the crowd is sitting in the front, I want the table in the back.

And that's just the first course.

For me, fine dining is fine as long as it's fast. I cannot sit still without getting sidetracked, which means my ears and eyes are tuned to every conversation and table except the one in front of me.

I am glued to the fat guy two tables down talking with his open mouth oozing white and red with cheesecake and strawberries. Or irritated by the skinny vegan woman with hennaed curly hair one seat over using her fingers as forks. Or uncomfortable about the middle-aged couple staring blankly at each other without a word or a touch between them. Or irked by the wife with the dreadful South African accent wearing a too tight dress, too much makeup, petting her smoothly tanned doctor husband under the table.

Perhaps they are all having a good time, but they are making me miserable.

Until our orders arrive.

You don't want to be my waitperson. Before he or she even gets the platter down on the service stand, I am asking for more napkins, a fizzier soda water, the music lowered, the smokers ejected.

You don't even want to be the Captain. He knows from experience what the pitfalls are. He knows I won't sit peacefully unless my back is to the wall and I am facing the room. I learn this position in Israel and cannot unlearn it in the States, a sort of basic training in the event of a terrorist attack. Don't expose your back. Always watch the room. Always sit in a corner. Keep your eye on the exit. Look out for suspicious packages left under chairs. Check your Uzi at the door. Eat and run.

Hit and run.

When I don't follow these rituals, I break into an absolute sweat.

The Captain tries to civilize me for years, to undo what was not done in Israel. *Manners*. The Captain is mostly patient, sometimes irritable, and he half succeeds in educating me.

Which reminds me of one of the Captain's favorite jokes:

A tourist goes to a grocery store in Moscow.
"Excuse me," she says, "I'd like to buy a pound of sausage."
"WHAT'S SAUSAGE?" the Russian shouts.
The tourist next visits a butcher in Rome.
"Excuse me, I'd like to buy a pound of sausage."
"What's a pound?" The Italian is confused.
The tourist finally visits a butcher in Tel Aviv.
"Excuse me, do you have any sausage in this country?"
The Israeli butcher stares her down impatiently.
"WHAT'S *EXCUSE ME*?"

Eventually I, too, become a stickler for propriety, especially if it involves everyone else.

I make my daughter eat with a knife and fork, European style. I make her place a napkin on her lap and wait until we are all seated before she begins. She learns to bring the food to her mouth via the silverware, not her mouth to the plate via her nose. She chews with small bites. She drinks the milk, not guzzles the gallon. Elbows are banished from the table, along with tooth picking and nail biting. If the phone rings, we do not automatically leap up. She asks to be excused even if she doesn't always wait for the answer. When her friends join us for dinner, they are expected to perform in the same way. Sometimes I have to remind them to work from the outside in with the silverware and that the plate below their plate is a service plate and isn't for the dessert. Because they are high-school juniors, they catch on.

I usually stand on ceremony if the Captain is heading the table and even follow the rules myself unless we're eating at my house and I'm the cook. Then there are loopholes—like sneaking chicken thighs to the dog pleading desperately at my feet, or getting up in the middle of dessert to lie down on the couch because I've had enough.

After years of heavy indoctrination, it is fitting to note that I still dine with disaster. Only by now the Captain tells me I am the terrorist.

TIE-BREAKERS

Things the Captain Teaches Me:

1. How to tie a clove hitch. (Wait. I forget.)
2. How to let the waiter know I'm done eating. (Place knife and fork together to the side of the plate.)
3. How to cook a rare steak filet with pepper sauce. (Sear the meat first with Lea & Perrins.)
4. How to sleep through the night with him in the same bed. (Take sleeping pills.)
5. How to throw a party that everyone shows up at. (Make it a big studio production.)
6. How to walk clients to the door. (Tell them "I'll walk you out" before they get too comfortable.)
7. How to say your name when you answer the phone. (Captain!)
8. How to handle martinis. (Don't finish the first one.)

9. How to handle raising a teenager. (Go sailing.)
10. How to say "No." (Do it by phone.)

Things I Teach the Captain:
1. How to jump through airport security lines in Tel Aviv. (Let me do the talking in Hebrew.)
2. How to finish other people's sentences. (Let me do the talking in English.)
3. How to pack. (Fold the shirts without the hangers.)
4. How to make linguine and clam sauce. (Use fresh basil.)
5. How sixties women are not fifties women. (Sex is not a chore.)
6. How to juggle seven things at the same time. (Ask me to do it.)
7. How to ask for directions. (Use your rest room stops wisely.)
8. How to make peace with his family. (Dial the international operator.)
9. How to say "I love you." (Tell him first.)

Why I Love Him:
1. He saves the day.
2. He makes every minute an adventure.
3. He tries incredibly hard to get it right.
4. He's kind and warmhearted.
5. He signs his trust fund over to his less able brother.
6. He takes charge when I give up.
7. He looks sexy in sweats.
8. He looks grand in a tuxedo.
9. He lights up a room.
10. His eyes light up when he sees me.

11. He is strong.
12. He is capable.
13. He is the only man I almost respect.

Why He Loves Me:

I don't think he really does.

SOME CRITICAL DETAILS

BOSTON AND THE CAPE

I don't know the Captain is a star athlete when we first order drinks. I think he's just an advertising film director. I certainly am not the cheerleader type. Maybe that's the trick. But I can see right away he is a natural leader and is naturally followed. He makes it his business to be well liked and backs it up by keeping his word. *"Watch me,"* he says.

Still I don't believe he is serious when he tells me, *"When I retire, I'm going sailing."*

Retirement seems a long way off. However, I should have noticed the nautical signs are already locked in place: his character is already Neptune-like—strong-willed, stubborn, and determined. I watch as his arty gray-flecked beard and collar-length whitening hair get thinner, shorter, and more seafaring as the years move on. Even his skin starts to lick salty.

When he first starts reading the Captain Horatio Hornblower series and subscribes to obscure ham-radio magazines, I am intrigued. He seems to want to know everything about everything, and especially how to do it himself. I never have to look anything up. He reminds me of a dog-eared-paged encyclopedia on photography, sailing, physics, radios, mutual funds, politics, history, writers, geography, weather, and on and on. And what he doesn't know he finds out and tells me whether I want to know or not.

He calls me a wounded bird when we first meet, but I can see he's as hurt as I am. I can see it in his eyes. They smile a lot from the corners out, like the tearstained eyes of my approval-seeking dog. When he is not threatened, he is calmly rational, and enormously helpful with advice in the big-picture details. He can be soft, warm, tender, romantic.

But the years of hurt are right there, just below the surface. I don't even need to dig to draw blood. His childhood, blurred in a swirl of embassy parties, top hats, tails, and starched-white collars propping up formal manners—credentials confirmed by engraved calling cards left on polished sterling-silver trays at the grand entrance hall—is glamorous only in the fairy-tale rendition. The reality is ruthless and cold. When the last guests depart and the heavy door shuts as the clock strikes midnight, things don't look as pretty. Behind the drawing-room curtains, the pecking order is well established. Critical reviews are mixed with one final nightcap, and then it's the cat that claws the dog that bites the baby birds that are caged in the house that Uncle Sam builds. And it is one more unhappy childhood.

Still there is a practiced quality to the Captain's good nature and polished performance from years of experience being the overachieving first son of an old-world-style European diplomat father, a Southern debutante mother, an Irish-immigrant-grandfather-turned-railroad-baron who brings his own train when he visits. Sometimes I think the idea of the Captain is greater than the reality of him. When I get confused, we fight.

The credentials are grand, but that's not the main attraction. In fact, his background is his Achilles' heel. To make peace with his patrician past, he breaks bread with peasants. He moves to a working-class town and puts on a blue denim shirt. He talks democratic but votes independent. He hates ties and jackets (except blue blazers), socks, and lace-up shoes. Formality makes him turn anxious with insecurity once the party is over, although until the door shuts and the guests depart, his manners are impeccable and he is quite the gentleman. Then I find out I do not behave like a lady. He tells me I say all the wrong things. I sit down when I should stand up. The freezer is too full. There's not enough ice. I interrupt him when he's talking. I always need to be the center of attention. I am not paying enough attention to him.

As the fight escalates, he storms out the door and leaves me behind to clean up the mess. I never really understand what happens. Two days of silence go by until I break down and show up at his house in the middle of the night to apologize.

"I'm sorry," I say.

We end up in bed, and start the dance steps all over again.

I think he needs a lot of love.

But so do I.

It's a match.

BIRDS-OF-PARADISE

After a few years of prodding, the Captain nervously organizes a formal introduction to his father, now enjoying tax-free retirement living with his second wife on the French Riviera. The Captain has been warming his father up for five days before my arrival, but I know his expectations are not high.

"My father didn't like my first wife because she wore pants," he mentions.

I wear a smart black dress.

We are to have cocktails precisely at 6 P.M. at the ambassador's residence, a Belle Époque penthouse apartment overlooking the Côte d'Azur.

Before our entrance, we dash into an expensive-looking florist's across the boulevard to organize a bouquet delivery to follow up our visit. After some discussion, I art-direct an arrangement of exotic tropical flowers, including four stalks of majestic bright red-and-orange flaming birds-of-paradise from the island of Mauritius, two rare South African proteas, a fan of jungle ferns mixed with yellow-striped elephant grass, and one deep violet orchid from Tahiti.

It is exactly 6 P.M.

The Ambassador and his second wife, whom I immediately see is a Duchess of the English tea-rose variety, greet us cordially at the front-door entrance. The Captain's father is dressed to the nines in a three-piece autumn-weight black wool suit. A white silk hankie is smartly tucked into the lapel pocket of his French-tailored double-breasted jacket. The Ambassador, almost ninety, still cuts a tall, handsome figure. Although the Captain is wearing suitcase-creased khaki pants, a just-ironed blue-striped shirt, worn boat shoes, and is hiding behind a film director's beard that needs a trim, I can see where he gets his looks.

At the gate of the stairwell, the Duchess smiles evenly and waits until her husband says:

"Well, shall we go in?"

A strident woman clearly to the English manor born, the Duchess floats regally over the threshold, barely rustling the hem of her Queen Elizabeth–style pastel floral-print dress and white low-heeled pumps. Her legs are long, her bone structure elegant, her hair coiffed into a halo of brown and gray around her faintly lined, gently powdered English complexion. If I didn't know she is in her late sixties, I could see her still lobbing tennis balls over the net and winning.

"Oh, it's quite lovely here," I compliment, noticing the pewter vases in the entrance hall filled with soft peaches-and-cream roses carefully camouflaging the tropical brilliance of the French Riviera. *"Like an English garden."*

"You Americans do tend to enjoy the color black," she remarks with a short glance at my dress.

The Captain is holding a matching smile on his face and stands poised to escort the Duchess into the spacious, yellow-tinted drawing room carpeted with a plush pale blue-and-ivory silk Chinese Oriental. Raw yellow Chinese silk fabric dresses the walls, bathing the room in a buttercup glow. A spotlight focuses on a group of dark Dutch Master oils hanging in heavy gilt frames.

There isn't a primary color in the entire place.

Before he settles into his silk-striped *soie de Lyon* upholstered armchair, the Ambassador offers me a tour of the penthouse. The Captain's eyebrows lift and signal me to proceed, but with caution.

The Ambassador personally escorts me through another parquet-floored hallway, brushing past pale champagne-colored tea roses sitting in a polished silver urn. He shows me the medieval Cluny tapestry draped behind a study door, a present from the Captain's late mother. He points out a set of ancient Ming-dynasty scrolls bequeathed to the Duchess by her wealthy late second husband, who I am also told leaves her a jade palace in China before the country turns red. He winds me through bisqued rooms of soft caramels perfumed with the scent of long-stemmed antique-white dinner roses.

His fingers trace over Louis XVI marquetry, Duncan Phyfe tables, English silver trays, a weighty eighteenth-century family Bible opened to show the lineage of his ancestors. I take a peek at the decades of marriage entries and am surprised to see the Ambassador's mother and I share the same first name. Only I'm not recorded.

The Ambassador tours me on through his personal study. Above a delicate mahogany French escritoire inset with a deep purple glass inkwell and one marble green-colored fountain-pen, the Captain's father directs me to a bookshelf neatly lined with black leather-bound diaries, faithfully recording in exacting fountain-pen script, the historical moments of his century-spanning diplomatic life.

I can see the Captain's problem with his childhood—why Oriental carpets, heavy furniture, and weighty titles make him anxious. But I like the old man anyway, even if he had been his country's diplomatic representative to Hitler's Berlin in 1933. I think he must have a lot of stories to tell. I am itching to read the journals.

The old Ambassador sighs. His thick-veined hands pull out a leather diary and flip the pages.

"It's all in here," he says.

I am interested.

"Did you ever make any world-altering decisions you regret?" I pry despite the Captain's warning not to ask too many questions.

"Yes," the Captain's father answers, catching me by surprise. And he tells me a secret.

He tells me he is one of the seven members of the United Nations committee appointed to divide Palestine into two separate states in 1947.

I am very interested.

He tells me how he sits in a small, overheated, windowless room in Flushing Meadows, New York, before the UN building is even an architectural plan, charged with drawing a line down the map of Palestine, cutting through towns and cities and mountains, dividing Jews from Arabs.

"We didn't even have a proper map," he confides. "No one on the committee had ever been to Palestine. We had seven days to carve out a state."

He tells me there is a map of the Holy Land printed on the last page of his family Bible—a Bible printed one hundred years earlier in 1848, marking the places of Jesus, the holy sites, the cities of the Old and New Testaments. The same Bible that now sits on his Louis XVI escritoire.

He tells me how he locks the door on the committee in Flushing Meadows and instructs them to sit still until he returns. How his driver races him into the city, where he unearths the family Bible from packed cartons of books in his hotel room. How he copies the map, enlarges it to a working size, then mounts it on the wall of the secret meeting room, where the six committee members are still waiting with their pencils, erasers, and scissors.

They draw lines. They cut up the map. They circle biblical cities. They crisscross through mountains and deserts. They divide neighbors from neighborhoods, cousins from grandparents, villagers from villages, farmers from fields. Fridays from mosques, Saturdays from synagogues. They have no idea what they are doing, or that what they do will never be undone without bloodshed.

"Imagine dividing Palestine in 1948 with a map from the Bible? For this, I am sorry." He shakes his head. "Not that it would have made any difference."

His revelation stuns me.

I think of my own family caught by the machine guns of Hitler's Germany. Their march from death camps in Poland to refugee ships in Italy. Jumping into the breaking surf to reach the coast of Haifa only to be swept up by waves of British patrols and sent to detention camps on Cyprus.

And here I stand facing the Captain's father, as righteous as Michelangelo's frescoed God in the Sistine Chapel, pointing the very finger of life that creates the State of Israel.

It is a complicated history.

And only one half of the story.

I think of my Jordanian friends, Palestinian exiles, their olive groves bearing fruit on the wrong side of the border. The humiliating shakedowns at checkpoints. The second-class citizenship. The seething resentment. Exacting inexact revenge.

I want to tell the Ambassador it does make a difference.

But the Duchess announces it is time for refreshments.

Opening sliding-glass doors, the Ambassador steps me outside onto a sweeping wraparound balcony ten floors higher than the ground the elegant Belle Époque building is rooted on. The change of climate clears the topic of conversation.

It is a beautiful balcony, only the grand view to the French blue sea is shuttered by a guardrail of towering Mediterranean cedars of Lebanon planted side by side in terra-cotta floor pots. Like military guards standing at round-the-clock attention, the firs spiral skyward, chests out, heads narrowing up to fine points.

"But you can hardly see the view!" I sputter.

The Captain, escorting the Duchess carrying a tray of crystal sherry glasses, throws me a meaningful look. Then I remember the Ambassador is afraid of heights. I know this only because the Captain is also afraid of heights.

While the Captain and his father huddle close to the balcony entrance doors sipping cocktails, I cover my words by hanging over the side rail, looking for an unblocked vista of any kind.

"Look!" I call, pointing across a dozen rooftops through a space in the trees, "Isn't that an Alexander Calder mobile on the roof over there? See the bright red, yellow, blue spherical colors? It must be a Calder." My tone is one of awe.

"Dreadful, isn't it?" remarks the Duchess. "Imagine putting that clothesline up on such a magnificent skyline. And the colors . . . so absolutely garish."

I swallow and nod.

The tropical medley of primary-colored flowers is due to be delivered in one hour.

The rest of the visit is resituated to the safety of the drawing room, where we are now seated on a rare set of delicate-legged French Empire hand carved chairs with Napoleon-blue-and-gold-leafed fleurs-de-lis painted backs. The conversation moves with the slow motion of a broken oven timer. I am desperate to escape and stop the florist before it is too late.

We chitchat about the heirless prince and his unlikely marriage prospects. About the declining manners in the members-only restaurant at the Royal Yacht Club. About the latest new-money upstarts moving into town. About the high cost of living in a tax-free climate. That the help isn't what it used to be. That the Ambassador's valet talks too much, the cook is getting too familiar.

The Duchess asks a few polite questions as to my line of work. I explain about art directors and clients and make sure to add a few supportive sentences about the talented Captain shooting for all the big-budget, five-star accounts.

"*I don't understand what my son does for a living, anyway!*" declares the Ambassador with an undiplomatic wave of dismissal.

The Captain looks pained.

"Finish your drink, darling," calms the Duchess. "You know it's almost time for dinner."

I move the conversation into her territory.

"Didn't you find it difficult to leave your family behind in England when you moved here?" I ask the Duchess, wondering how the Captain and I can exit as gracefully.

"Actually, I haven't given it much thought." She snaps closed the conversation.

The Captain struggles to hold his back still, but I can see it is aching him. He hasn't stirred from his erect position on the delicate-legged chair for the entire hour. He makes a slight movement, an almost invisible twist to the left, to unlock the cramp in his thigh muscle.

The Ambassador is eyeing his fifty-year-old son with increasing agitation. *"Sit still!"* he orders.

The Captain can't. He adjusts his spine with a sudden spasm.

And an uncontrollable lurch.

The chair leg splits from its corner and the French Empire collapses.

The Captain spills onto the parquet with a thump.

"My Louis XVI chair!" barks the old man.

"It can be mended, dear," soothes his second wife.

"And you?" she asks, after the Captain rights himself.

We are saved by the bell chiming on the ormolu clock.

"Hurry," I urge as we make our escape out of the gilt elevator cage that has just descended ten floors to the lobby. "We've got to get to the florist before they close!"

We are just in time.

The uniformed footman is on his way out the polished brass-and-mahogany shop door carrying an eye-popping display of tropical flowers sealed in a swath of sheer cellophane.

After a half-hour delay, the footman is on his way across the boulevard again.

Only this time he is cradling an English garden of soft butter-cream-colored roses.

THE MIDDLE

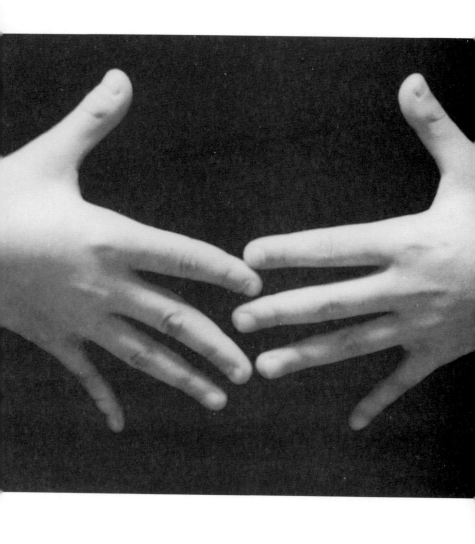

BERMUDA TRIANGLES

AROUND

Relationships never get less complicated as they get older.

Right from the beginning, even our basic triangle has triangles.

Somebody is always pointing in an opposite direction. The tugs on each point come in circles, and go around and around, never getting resolved, until they get lost somewhere in the background for a few days, a month, a year, or five.

But there's always an angle that needs to be righted. And always someone who feels wronged.

The first triangle is the most obvious:

CONFIGURATION #1: *the Captain, me, my daughter*
RECONFIGURATION #2: *me, my daughter, the Captain*
RECONFIGURATION #3: *my daughter, me, the Captain*
RECONFIGURATION #4: *my daughter, the Captain, me*

She loves him, sort of, but she loves me more.

He loves me sort of. He loves her, sort of. But he loves himself more.

I love her, but not with him.

I love him, but not with her.

I would love to love all of them together, but he won't take us on as a whole, only in parts.

WHITE GLOVES

THE BARN

There is a rambling, authentic, two-story Cape barn behind the now restored Cape house, which lists to the left in good weather. The antique, weathered shingled barn has seen better days. The Captain uses the bottom half of the barn for storage for oversize sails that don't fit the boat, old oars, a wooden Cape dory with dry rot, black plastic trash barrel bags filled with empty tonic-water cans, and bottles needing to be recycled or taken to the dump. Sundry half-gallon tins of expensive white, marine oil-based paint, the kind that makes the boat's cabin surfaces slick white, and tall cans of high-gloss, white enamel spray paint line the splattered shelves.

The second half of the ground level, devoted to the Captain's unheated, uninsulated workshop, is lit by one dangling naked lightbulb. Inside is an electric radial arm-saw, a long workbench table supported by four sawhorses, odd lots of paint thinner, dozens of different-sized screw drivers, drill bits, wrenches, putty knives, hammers, hand saws, and fragments of wood left over from various building projects he is always in the middle of.

The second floor of the barn is more intriguing.

With barn boards askew like teeth knocked out in a nine-round fight, the aged walls hold a room and a loft area together by sheer willpower.

The second floor of the barn is entered up a tilty, plank-wide, barn-board staircase located at the deep end of the garage area. The narrow stairs twist up like an arthritic finger past a small broken, four-paned glass window that gives a dusty view of the back brambles and weedy mound of a vegetable garden gone to seed. *"I'll garden when I'm seventy,"* he says.

The stairs exit directly into the first chamber, a large, grime-coated, many-windowed room with unsanded wide pine-board floors that once held the secret recipe for rose-hip preserves. Hundreds of cobwebbed, empty glass mason jars still nestle in rusty rimmed, wooden keg-sized barrels that look desperate enough to fling themselves over Niagara Falls.

The best part of this room is the secret trapdoor in the floorboards.

The story that comes with the house claims the original owner's eight-year-old daughter falls through the trap door down to the garage level and lands on her head on the concrete foundation, making her slow-witted for the rest of her life; or she dies. I can't remember. But I make sure the Captain makes sure the trapdoor is nailed safely shut because my daughter is just about the same age as the daughter of legend and probably as curious. We tell her the story often in hopes of curbing her appetite for trouble. She is also aware of the ghost that floats around and haunts the place, and her fear keeps her on her toes.

On good days, my daughter and her weekend Cape friends use the upper floor of the barn for a clubhouse, a theater, hide-and-seek, and animal husbandry. The girls know the bottom rooms belong to the Captain and are off-limits. They respect this.

There is safety in numbers. So when the girls are duking it out in the barn, fighting over who gets the lead role in a play they are concocting, the Captain and I are across the lawn in the newly renovated house, breathing sighs of relief upstairs in the master bedroom.

There is nothing better than a one-hour Sunday-afternoon nap after cracking the crossword puzzle. Especially if the Captain joins me.

My daughter doesn't believe in naps. She likes to keep moving. She is annoyed with these weekend siestas. She feels left out, at loose ends. She is not the kind of child who can entertain herself by kicking off her sneakers and curling up on her bed reading my favorite childhood book, *Magic by the Lake*.

She wants the magic *now*.

It's obvious there's going to be trouble.

Even though we are having a nap, I am awake to all possibilities. Lying flat on his back on his half of the bed, the Captain looks like his eyes are closed, but his fingers are crossed.

First comes the knock on the door, then the burst into the room.

"Did you take your shoes off downstairs?" he asks without a pause, flicking his eyes open like a light switch.

"Yes. *See?*" She is bouncing on all ten toes. "The girls went home. They don't want to play with me anymore."

There is a well-rehearsed whine to her voice. She stretches her full, juicy lips even wider than her Chiclet-sized white teeth.

"Can you play on your own, then, and give us an hour for a nap?" I plead. "Then later, we'll take a bike ride to the beach."

It seems I am always begging her for sleep.

"Can I paint?" She is hopeful. She runs the teeth of her pink, plastic headband back and forth through the crown of her sunny locks she won't let be cut since the age of two.

"Ask the Captain."

"Well? Please, can I paint something in the barn?"

She is now dancing with the door to the master bedroom, swinging it back and forth on its brass hinges. "Well, can I?"

The Captain is suspicious. His eyebrows rise.

"Like what?" he asks.

She is not too sure.

"Please, can I?"

"Okay." He relents uneasily.

"But just don't paint the barn." His voice is fatherly but firm.

I am hoping this creative moment will endure the hour. I like it that she wants to paint. I leave a whole rainbow of tempera watercolors up in her barn clubhouse for theater-production sets. This is the first time she expresses an interest in using them without me art-directing.

"Have fun." I add. "We'll be awake in an hour."

"And remember what I said." The Captain underscores his position by propping his hands up behind his head to give her a last look. *"Just don't paint the barn."*

She disappears.

This is what she does in the hour:

It is getting darker inside the barn because the late-afternoon sun is fading across the sky. The one dangling light-bulb in the Captain's workshop is casting a spooky shadow on the walls. The planking that outlines the aged pine doors in the workroom and up the stairs between the second-story inner chamber and the loft is dark, stained with two hundred years of time.

My daughter thinks it is time to brighten up the place. She doesn't have to look too far for a solution. Her eyes light on the row of white enamel spray-paint cans sitting on the shelf in the Captain's storage room. White is bright.

She uncaps a brand-new can of oil-based, high-gloss white paint, shakes the can up and down to the beat of the steel ball rattling inside.

She stops shaking.

The ball settles.

Then she lets it rip.

With a steady aim, she spray paints the doorways, the thresholds, the sills, the wood bordering the doors. She is thinking this is not the actual barn. This is only the molding around the doors.

When the can is almost empty, she stops, stands back, and surveys the results.

My daughter is impressed with her work. Her teeth flash a self-congratulatory smile as white as the shiny paint on the woodwork.

"Oh, it looks so much better," she thinks out loud with supreme satisfaction.

She finishes the project with one last solid spurt. Oil paint dribbles from the nozzle onto her hands and feels sticky. She rubs her fingers with a spotty rag, but it doesn't budge the color. Studying the smeared effect, she decides she doesn't like the white polka-dot splatters on her skin. It looks unfinished.

She rectifies the problem by spraying both hands from the tips of her ten chewed fingernails up the entire length of her forearms until the skin is completely saturated with paint.

"White gloves!" she exclaims out loud, delighted with herself.

Admiring her debutante-formal, up-to-her-elbows, shiny, skin-tight white gloves, she prances around the gloomy barn with glow-in-the-dark hands looking for applause, because if she claps for herself, she'll stick.

But the audience is sleeping.

The hour passes quickly. She knows it's time to clean up.

Her white hands stick to the plastic cap of the can.

Her fingers stick to her hair when she scratches her head.

She thinks to scrub clean with soap and water, but the only sink is in the kitchen bathroom in the main house.

Holding her hands up in front of her, she exits the barn.

She crosses the lawn to the back door.

With her white gloves on, she opens the natural pine French doors to the kitchen. She grasps the outside brass handle, enters the kitchen, and pulls the doors shut behind her. She doesn't forget to kick off her sneakers on the hooked rug before trotting to the bathroom door. Her white-gloved fingers wrap around the bathroom doorknob. She moves to the sink, twists on the brushed steel faucets, digs into the white porcelain soap dish. She settles her gloved hands into the corner sink basin to soak but quickly discovers oil and water don't mix. Dripping wet, the gloves move over to the washer/dryer machines to reach for a fluffy clean navy-blue bath towel, then to the inside bathroom doorknob to get out.

Just about now she realizes white gloves don't wash off. It's as if she'd been born with them on.

She looks at the kitchen clock. It is almost an hour later, but not quite.

High-gloss-oil-paint fingertips print their signature throughout the Captain's new/old house, tracking through the kitchen, living room, hallway, fingerprinting the polished oak banister as she pulls herself upstairs to knock once more on the master-bedroom door.

"Captain? Mom?" she calls behind the door.

Through my half nap, I sense trouble.

I tap the Captain on his shoulder and release him from a snore.

"Yes?" he answers, at once wide-awake.

"The paint won't come off my hands." Her voice is muffled through the closed door, but the intent knocks through.

As if caught dozing through his ship watch, the Captain leaps up, pulls the bedroom door open wide, and catches her midswipe at the doorknob.

She holds her shiny white-gloved hands up like Cinderella at the ball with the clock just striking midnight.

"I can't get the paint off," she tells him.

I think he knows this.

He is very calm, very still. Controlled. He doesn't raise his voice (I do). He doesn't shout (I do). He simply marches her back downstairs to the front-hall closet, where he keeps indoor tools, telephone books, and hardware, and pulls a gallon of turpentine down from the overhead shelf.

The two of them are missing for another hour.

When they surface, her hands are scrubbed a raw red and smell like the devil soaked in kerosene.

When I dare descend to help make dinner, I never see a white paint spot, a finger mark, an unexplained streak of white anywhere in the house. All telltale signs are wiped clean with rags dipped in paint thinner.

But a visit to the barn is more illuminating.

It takes days for the oily white paint to dry around the damp barn doors and sills.

It takes years for my like-me daughter to confide she didn't mean to do it even though she did it.

She tells me she is like a magnet. She just can't help herself. The forces are too great. Because the Captain said not to, she just had to.

My daughter doesn't like to be left out.

I understand her perfectly.

GERTRUDE

. . . is a duck, who I'd like to say waddles into our lives down the Cape one summer's evening, but she isn't old enough to have hips. She is a foundling, perhaps only a day-or-two-old duckling who misplaces her mother and nestles instead in the downy feathers of the sea grass on the front lawn.

My daughter cartwheels over her terrified fetal duck form about six times before she notices a tiny nib of beak snipping at the corners of the grass blades like blunt scissors.

The duck doesn't have a chance.

Flicking her ponytail from upside down to right side up, my daughter tumbles to her feet, scoops the bird up, nearly squeezing the feeble breath out of the duckling's wobbly neck in the excitement of her discovery. Squealing, she races around to the back deck, throws open the kitchen door, forgets to take off her sneakers, and catapults the baby duck onto the dinner platter of littleneck steamers the Captain is just setting on the table.

My daughter is not at all concerned about the Captain's dinner decorum. She is bringing a guest without an invitation and demands he set an extra plate. The duckling is not much bigger than a dinner roll, doesn't take up a lot of space, but its sideways paddling around the maple-wood table surface on flat, miniature webbed feet demand our complete, awed attention.

I know the Captain wants to say, "Take that duck off the table, we're eating," but he is a softy inside where it counts, and instead, fans his giant hands into a pen to keep the baby bird from plopping off the edge of the table.

The duckling stumbles through the first course like a cabin boy after an illicit swig of bootleg whiskey, tippling left and right as it makes its way around the forks and knives and white plates in complete confusion. Despite the telltale thumping of the little heart, the duckling looks exactly like an old-fashioned, metal windup mechanical toy duck whose turnkey is stuck in the On position.

My own heart pushes out from my chest in motherly instinct. I am dying to hold the lost soul in my warm hands, to cross the duckling from the kitchen plates to safety. However, my daughter claims immediate control of the birth certificate and proudly holds the baby duck up like a nurse supervisor behind the window in the maternity ward—*look, but don't touch.*

The Captain gently interrupts this presentation with a few words of wisdom.

"Where's the mother?" he asks.

The answer is silence, mixed with a nervous shuffle of feet on the braided hooked rug under the table.

"It lost its mother." My daughter is experienced with this concept. She jumps up and down at her seat, clutching the bird possessively against her cheek, daring anyone to de-mother her rights to adoption.

"It's not an *it*. It is a she, and her name is Gertrude," I announce with absolute certainty.

All eyes turn to me.

The Captain blinks an amused smile. He is waiting for an explanation, which he knows will be outrageous.

My daughter accepts the name without hesitation.

"Can Gertrude stay?" she asks. "Can she?" She throws him a bright smile. "The Captain can build her a cage and make a bed to keep her warm. Look, she's cold!"

She and I turn our eyes simultaneously in the same direction and give the Captain an accusatory stare.

"She needs a lightbulb," the Captain offers cautiously, feeling the rope tighten around his conscience.

It's a bright idea. Really, I never would have thought of it. I can see he is also warming to the duck, because when my daughter passes Gertrude on to him with an outstretched arm, he circles his open fist around her little downy breast as if he is holding a jigger of room-temperature Scotch.

Gertrude loves him. She settles right in and immediately takes a nap in the Captain's cupped hand.

"I'll serve," I say, hoping the Captain will stay put. I dish out the steamers, the broth, the butter, the lemons.

While Gertrude sleeps in his left hand, the Captain works out the tender steamed clams from their opened shells with his right, soaks the sand off in the broth, dips a few necks into the drawn lemon butter, and manages to eat, drink, and mother the duckling, all at the same time.

"Why the name?" he finally asks. He settles into the curved back of his white plastic kitchen chair, left arm still extended on the table, left hand still bedding the duck. He knows he could be in for a long story.

"She looks like a Gertrude," I answer.

In truth, I give her that name because she reminds me of the friendly, white, down-comforter-quality pet goose from *Journey to the Center of the Earth* who gets eaten for breakfast by a greedy villain scientist when the hungry expedition gets trapped deep inside the core of an Icelandic volcano. I tell my daughter and the Captain the story, unwrapping the details like the foil cover on an after-dinner mint, trying to refresh their memories of Hans, the able-bodied Nordic guide, and his devoted duck, Gertrude, who follows after him literally to the ends of the earth, until she ends up in a trail of white plucked feathers and drops of fowl blood.

They get the idea.

"I'll clear," I offer once we're through with the last gory giblets. I am hoping the Captain will still stay put and keep the duck safe in his hands.

My daughter asks to be excused. She wants to show Gertrude off to the girls down the road.

"Leave the duck here," I suggest. "She's had a hard day. Bring the girls over instead."

The Captain nods.

My daughter is gone, leaving the kitchen door open wide to all mosquitoes and summer flying insects also attracted by the idea of warm lightbulbs.

Day is done. It's growing dark outside. The fireflies, cicadas, grasshoppers chirp in the glow of the twinkling stars and almost full moon.

The Captain is also tired. But he is stuck holding the goods. It doesn't seem to bother him too much. He moves out from the table, duck in hand, and steps around the partition from the kitchen into the living room, laying himself horizontally on the cushions of the striped blue-and-white-ticking couch.

He doesn't spill the duck. His fist still warms Gertrude neatly like an incubator. Head on the end pillow, feet crossed out on the far couch arm, he is asleep in the time it takes me to turn on the dishwasher.

I love him for this.

The moment of serenity is just that, a moment.

The back door, only just shut, springs open again, this time launching a gaggle of girls into the kitchen.

"Where's Gertrude?" my daughter demands, eyes darting with suspicion. She sweeps her heavy bangs from her brow with chewed fingernails. I see fear cross her path for a brief second, as if she is caught out fibbing in front of her weekend friends.

I point them into the living room. "Take your shoes off, girls."

The Captain's last snort shakes him awake. He looks up into the four pairs of eyes looking down at him, or rather, looking at the sleeping duck he is still holding in his left hand.

"See, I told you," my daughter brags. She is all teeth. "The Captain is building Gertrude a cage with a lightbulb. She's going to live with us in Boston out on the back patio."

This is an interesting thought, but unlikely. We have cats

that eat birds for dessert. I remind my daughter about Tweetie, her first pet bird, who sings his last song outside on the patio before he croaks.

"This is a Cape Cod mallard," the oldest girl, a preteen who is a bit bossy, announces. "It's not fair to take the duck to the city. I know all about ducks. We raise them." She throws out the Latin nomenclature for the species, but to me the duck looks just like a duck.

"Yeah," pipes up the second-oldest girl, less sure. She slouches in the corner like a skinny, tin-handled inverted spoon. Maybe she wishes she could be taken to the city instead of the duck.

"Anyway, I know where the mother is." It's clear the bossy girl likes being the agent of powerful information. "She's in the river behind the miniature golf course with her baby duck-lings. I saw them this afternoon. You have to bring her back." She stares down my daughter with narrow eyes that in two more years will be caked with heavy black eyeliner.

The golf course lies at the foot of the hill beyond the curve of our country lane. A salt-marsh river runs through it. The ex-planation is plausible.

My daughter's bright moon face falls. Her quivering full lips collapse like a popped red balloon into the cleft of her square chin. Her pained, wide blue eyes, giant with enormous black pupils, fill with tears that could drown a dormouse. The moment is ripe with emotion.

My daughter knows what is the right thing to do.

She snatches the duck from the Captain's hand, runs up-stairs with the bird locked in her grasp, three stairs at a time. Behind the just slammed bedroom door, she hides in her room.

The sobs break even the heart of the walls.

The Captain says he will go up and speak with her. But I know it's my place. I am her mother. I also know exactly what to say.

I ask the other girls to wait outside on the front lawn. I give my daughter a few private minutes alone behind closed doors.

Then I go upstairs.

When she lets me in, I cuddle her and Gertrude together on the narrow twin camp bed snuggled against the base of the pitched-roof Velux window.

"Remember how your father took you away from Mommy when you were just a little baby?" I rock her, twirling her ponytail around and around in my fingers. "Remember how I flew all across the world looking for you? Remember how scared you were to be lost from your mommy for so many months? Remember how happy you felt when Mommy finally found you after looking and looking for you everywhere? Don't you think Gertrude's mommy is worried sick about her?"

"I love Gertrude," my daughter sobs. Her hot cheeks are runny with salty tears and nose slime. *"It's my only duck."*

"You know the right thing to do," I tell her. "I know you know. But it's your choice. The Captain and I will be downstairs. You can tell us what you want to do when you're ready." I kiss her under the damp bangs stuck to her sweaty forehead, stroke Gertrude on her wobbly throat, and close the bedroom door quietly behind me.

My daughter appears five minutes later at the bottom of the stairs. With the duck.

She is ready.

We all put on our shoes. In the light of the moon, we traipse single file, one by one, the weekend girls first, my daughter in front of me with Gertrude tucked under her neck; I am next, the Captain is pulling up the rear, shining the way with a small pocket flashlight.

The staff at the miniature golf course is too busy with evening tourists hitting balls into sand traps to notice our parade across the back greens over the grassy hillock and footbridge down to the moving stream.

"Look!" cries the bossy girl, who knows the difference between ducks.

We follow her finger. A quacking mallard mother duck with six very baby goslings in tow is swimming up and down the river. Just like that. Up and down, down and up, retracing their paddles, as if the mother is looking for something much bigger than a bread crumb.

My daughter heaves her breath in a brave inhale. Gertrude is nuzzled under her neck, warm and fluffy.

But it is now time for her to go home. I can see Gertrude's mother is anxious.

My daughter moves down to the river's edge, holds one hand up like a school crossing guard, and orders everyone to stand back.

"*I can do it myself!*" she announces.

The Captain retreats into the shadows, the weekend girls lounge by the far edge of the stream. I stand behind her and wait.

My daughter says some private last words to her only duck.

I look at the stream and see the mother duck and her six goslings paddling along with the current, moving at a more determined clip.

I look again and recount. I've made a mistake. I see the mother duck and her one, two, three, four, five, six, seven goslings paddling along with the current, moving away from the miniature golf course at a more determined clip. Just like that.

I see my own daughter waving good-bye with a sad little hand.

And I love her for this.

SWEET SAILING

AT SEA

(Chapters to write but won't because you might think I had a good time:)
- The Boat
- Our First Voyage
- The Witch in the Lighthouse
- Sailing Stories
- Throwing Up—Upwind
- Lobster Pot Tangles
- Midnight Leaks
- Hurricane Hassles
- The Stuck-in-the-Pot White Plastic Plate
- Head Tales
- Lobster Tails
- Menus at Sea
- Bedtime Stories

NIGHT TALES

"There are two little girls lost at sea," I tell them, uncoiling the first chapter of a five-year bedtime story one evening when my daughter, the Captain, and I are snug in our bunk beds, anchored outside the harbor seawall of the Elizabeth Islands.

"Don't you remember where we last left them?

"They've been sailing for years and years, growing up and out of their too tight bathing suits, piloting their boat around the seven seas because they don't have an anchor to throw out; because they never learned how to motor into a harbor, grab a mushroom float buoy, tie a holding knot, find their way through the channel markers.

"They are alone at sea, forever it seems, from the day, that terrible day, their parents fell overboard on a slap of a tidal wave and disappeared into the rising tide and chalky fog.

"Sara Melindi is only five. Caravanessa is nine years old, but she is a brave girl and takes charge because now there are just the two of them. Caravanessa grabs the wheel. She drops the sails. She honks frantically on the foghorn. She cups her hand over her mouth and shouts through the wind,

" *'Papa! Mams!'*

"And Sara Melindi cries; her crimped yellow hair stringy with sea spray and salt, she holds on to the stretchy blue strap of Caravanessa's bathing suit, sticks one thumb into the open socket of her shorted-out mouth, and wails,

" *'MUMMMY!'*

"And the cry is eaten by a swooping seagull, snapped up in the wind, gulped, gone into thick air, swallowed like a crumb of bread, then dropped like a half-opened shell of an oyster back into the ocean.

"The girls stand side by side at the helm, alone in the thickening mist. The boat leaps over the waves, deep out to sea. And they are lost."

To be continued . . .

DISASTERS AT SEA

The Captain says he can never understand why his first two wives leave him, why he fights all the time with the women in his life. Why they are so angry.

I can tell you. And I don't even need to go that far back.

THE NOSE

We are not on his boat. We are riding on the passenger ferry to the island of Nantucket.

It is not summer. It is Christmas, our fourth together.

The iron-forged, triple-deck-enclosed steamship plows through the choppy gray winter waters from Hyannis to Nantucket through Vineyard Sound, carrying families home for the holidays or mixed breeds like us to celebrate Christmas in a cozy New England inn far removed from Christmases past. I choose this remote location for the Captain, my daughter, and myself to prevent igniting a moral crisis about whether or not I will allow a Christmas tree at the Cape house, which isn't much of a dilemma because the answer is *no*.

The ferry ride to Nantucket is a long three-hour trip. Our

car, hitching an easy ride, is parked on the auto deck below. The hatchback is packed with shiny gift-wrapped presents in weekend sailing bags brimming with bulky winter sweaters, boots, and down jackets.

The drone of the engines of the mammoth ferry lulls us along in our commuter seats in a hypnotic state. I am leaning against the solid shoulder of the Captain and he is leaning against the chair headrest, contentedly absorbed in the pages of Dodge Morgan's account of his solo, around-the-world sailing adventure. My daughter's head is nestled in my lap, thumb stuck in her mouth, drifting in and out of happy thoughts of sugarplums and what the Captain might have for her in one of those big bags, even though she's been told it's not her holiday.

By late afternoon, under heavy gray skies, the ferry groans into port and like a fat lady who has just removed her girdle, exhales us and the car onto the rain-slicked dock. We have no right to be tired, but we probably are. We've been up since the early morning. The drive down from Boston to Hyannis takes a good two hours, add in another hour for the wait to load the ferry, plus the three-hour sea voyage, and the bottom line is a very long day, all for a two-night holiday getaway.

In the packed car, the Captain drives us down the gangway from the ferry onto land. From the front passenger seat, I hold the local map and navigate our way through the narrow cobbled streets to the inn on the other side of town. There are no numbered day beacons, only street signs, so it's not that hard.

We drive into the center of Nantucket, an original New England whaling town perched out in the cold North Atlantic. Nantucket squeaks of scrimshaw, harpoons, and creaking white picket widow's walks at crow's nest height crowning stately sea-captain homes of red brick or white clapboard. The atmosphere is thick with rolling fog and gas lanterns and it is easy enough to imagine old Ahab himself limping down the cobblestone lanes on a frosty morning, tapping his wooden leg like a blind man with a cane as he makes his way from the ship's chandlery with provisions for the *Pequod* before he meets up with Moby-Dick.

This late afternoon, there is a Christmas excitement that catches our breath and my attention. The town is dressed for the holiday. Each upright, polished oak front door is festooned with holly wreaths and sprigs of dried cranberries. Elegant bay windows, draped with English antique white linen curtains or heavy red-and-gold velvet swags, are lit up by long bayberry or beeswax candles, the flickering flames dancing over and over one another in good cheer on each pane of glass. The church bell of the 1800s belfry is outpealing even the season's greetings of seagulls diving down for a peck at the popcorn and roast chestnuts stringing the fir Christmas tree in the town square. It is a scene from an antique Christmas postcard, only it's raining, not snowing.

It is two hours to Christmas Eve. I have an art director's urge to stop and explore the picture-perfect town first before all the stores shut down for Christmas dinner.

"Let's get out," I suggest, "and walk around."

The Captain freezes me with a look.

"*Why?*" he counters. His tone is testy. This is not the harbor. There are no boats docked on the main street. What is there to see?

"I want to look in the shops," I push. "In an hour, they'll be closed forever."

My daughter sticks with me, and he is outvoted.

"Fine. I'll wait in the car," he says.

The Captain is not being generous. He is rarely interested in window-shopping unless it's at a marina and the windows are portholes. I hate it when he tells me he'll wait in the car. It's like slamming the door shut on my curiosity. Usually I give in and say never mind, but now I don't feel like it. We are not likely to be in Nantucket on Christmas again soon.

"I'll go with you, Mommy," offers my daughter, who is probably hoping I'll buy her a present or a large salad.

"We need our jackets out of the trunk," I insist.

"I'll get them," the Captain offers without moving. He sulks at the wheel, not budging.

"No, I'll get them," I counter, in not such a nice tone of voice.

The race is on.

He pushes open the driver's door with the force of his shoulder. At the same time I get out of the passenger side and meet him head-to-head at the rear of the car.

The Captain unlocks the hatchback and lifts the door high up into the air. I hurry and push myself deep into the trunk and reach inside a sailing bag for our jackets. Rain is squeezing out fists of water from a plump cloud directly over the Captain's uncovered head.

He stands to the left, one arm holding the hatchback door in the air, keys still in the lock, while I dig in the boot, extracting a tangle of jacket arms from the loaded sailing bag. My daughter slips around out the back door and moves to watch the struggle from the curb.

It happens very quickly. So quickly, in fact, I don't even know which is the correct order of events.

1. Does it happen like this?

I grab the jackets and move from the trunk, head halfway out but not quite, nose forward. In a split second I change my mind and think I should also grab the umbrellas and duck back into the trunk to get them.

2. Or like this?

I grab the jackets and move out of the trunk completely, have second thoughts about the rain, and plunge my head, nose first, back into the trunk without pause to dig out umbrellas, just at the same exact moment as the Captain suddenly slams shut the hatchback door.

Either way, the result is the same.

Middescent, the downward smack of the hatchback door catches me right on the bridge of my nose. My mouth rounds into one short scream that does not sound like a Christmas carol. In that quick slice of time, I see stars on a canvas of black velvet and feel an instinctive flash of camaraderie with prize-fighters when they get a punch in the killer end of the nose right between the eyes. Only hatchback door edges are not padded like boxing gloves.

When I become aware of the bigger picture, I see the Captain outlined in white.

Horrified, he steps back while I teeter-totter against the car fender and shouts:

"Why do you always have to get in the way?"

"Why do you always have to be in control!"

"You should have told me you needed the umbrellas!"

"JESUS CHRIST!"

And he continues to shout, then abruptly stalks off down

the street and disappears into the fog blowing up from the corner.

My little daughter takes the hand that's not holding my face and gently leads me to the curb. I sink on the wet sidewalk, expecting a gush of blood and a night in the emergency room in Nantucket on Christmas Eve. When I look down at my hand, I am confused to find the nose is dry, especially considering the sound of the crack. I am now moving from stunned pain to raw anger.

The Captain is nowhere around.

I am devastated, hurt, furious the Captain leaves me just like that at a time like this. I cannot even comprehend the magnitude of his desertion. While I sit collapsed on the curb, cupping my bashed nose in my hand, my little daughter props me up.

"I'll take care of you, Mommy," she comforts.

Isn't it supposed to be the other way around?

A local policeman dressed as Santa Claus witnessing the event from the opposite street corner saves the day. He brings a Dixie cup of ice cubes from a nearby café, helps me chill the bridge of my nose with ice, and offers me a park bench to sit on after I dismiss his idea of an ambulance.

"Don't worry," he assures me, "your husband will come back. He needs a few minutes to collect himself because he is so upset."

Upset at what? Who's upset here?

It seems like forever before I realize I can take my daughter on to the inn by myself. The car keys are still in the hatchback door. My nose might be broken, but I am not crippled.

Just as I make the decision to move on, the Captain suddenly reemerges from back around the corner. He now seems to have himself under firm control.

"Are you okay?" he asks with a worry to his voice. He looks at me sheepishly.

I am still seeing stars, but my relief at his return is greater than the pain of my injury.

"I don't know," I mumble. "Would I know if my nose is broken?"

"You'd know," he answers, pointing to his own nose, thick with rugby-kicked experience.

"Do you need to go to the hospital?" he asks.

I am holding ice up to my right eye, which is working itself into a black-and-blue shiner, but I can still see out of it, and it will forever look at him a little distrustfully. "No, let's check into the hotel. I'd like to lie down."

He thinks it's a smart move. Something we should have done from the start.

The Captain turns solicitous when we get to the inn. He sweeps us and our bags into an elegant suite of rooms with an antique step-up, four-poster canopy bed, a gas-lit fireplace, and a sitting area connecting to a small inner chamber with a frilly twin hideaway daybed, perfect for a little girl.

He leaves me resting on my side of the bed and brings up more ice for my face, an orange juice for my daughter, and a rum and tonic for himself when he goes downstairs to confirm reservations for Christmas dinner.

When we settle in the queen-size canopy bed for the night, gas fire roaring, goose-down comforter plumped up, he rolls into my side, puts his arm gently around me, and whispers in my ear, *"That must have hurt."*

But that's all he says about the incident. We never talk

about why he storms off wildly at the curb, even though I have already forgiven him. Instead, I think he is more concerned the black-and-blue marks puffing up under my eye will look uncomfortably suspicious at breakfast.

On the morning of Christmas Day, tucked in bed, he surprises me with a leather-bound photo album of pictures he has secretly been taking of my daughter's Saturday-morning dance classes. The rich nutty-colored leather cover is stamped in gold with the title *Ballet Lessons*. His time and effort to record the moments of my daughter's first leaps, pliés, and relevés move me. The photos are black-and-white, simple prints, endearing. He looks at me for approval, but I hold back a full display of delight. I thank him with a kiss, tell him the album is beautiful, and share the pictures with my daughter, who is snuggled next to me in bed. Then I give him his present in return; a large monogrammed sailing bag filled with a treasure of books and an antique compass to sail by.

But somehow I never quite fully trust him to be around when there's serious trouble, even though we both understand that getting in the way of the car door is all my fault to begin with.

COCKROACHES

It is mid-February. The red is just fading off the hearts of Valentine's Day.

We are invited over for a good-bye dinner prepared by the Captain's senior studio assistant, who is moving on home to Montana. The Captain is honored that his senior assistant, usually the designated food stylist on the set, is cooking up this farewell gesture for him personally at his South End apartment. I have strict instructions to be dressed and ready to go in plenty of time.

After a few parking difficulties finding space between snowbanks, we arrive almost on time to an enthusiastic reception. We are ushered into an emptying flat, which our young host immediately rectifies by filling up four long-stemmed glasses with fine California wine. Drink in hand, the Captain talks and his senior assistant listens in rapt attention over half-filled moving boxes stacked in the living room.

The senior assistant's Blondie-look-alike art-director girlfriend and I are already in the kitchen swapping boyfriend tales. Though ten years separate us in age, we agree on almost everything. We talk about romance. She tells me how she cuts heart shapes out of the bread for her boyfriend's sandwiches on Valentine's Day. And how he doesn't notice. She tells me about missing being naughty, being shocking, passionate. Which is why, I am assuming, she is wearing a Madonna-like pointy leather bustier under a see-through mesh blouse this evening. But then nothing she does surprises me. What I really want to know is why he is moving to Montana? Why is she striking out instead for California? Is this truly an issue about exploring new job opportunities, or is it, in actuality, a breakup?

She tours me around the depleted apartment. In the empty-shelved bathroom I take a minute to glance in the mirror and adjust my lipstick. Through the corner of my eye, I am startled to see a lineup of tenement-size cockroaches, one brown, one black, one crunchy-backed and multicolored with antennae raised, creeping along the bathroom windowsill. It takes me a second to realize they are plastic, and I laugh.

"Take them," she donates. "I forgot to pack them."

"Really? Are you sure?"

She drops the three cockroaches in my hand.

"Thanks," I say. I am already visualizing them in their new home.

We move back to the kitchen to check on the exquisitely prepared medallions of lamb resting on the cutting board. I fiddle with the cockroaches in my palm, then set them out in a group on the counter, legs down, antennae up.

They are arresting insects. The cockroaches catch our breath one more time because they look so true-to-life. We both look at the insects. We both eye the meat. I eye her. She eyes me. Our eyebrows inch up our foreheads as the idea turns from a napkin scribble into reality.

"Don't you think the wild rice could use a little extra something?"

I have no idea she can cook so well.

I hand her the brown insect with the behemoth antennae and it disappears immediately into the rare end of the cut. With great attention to detail and design, she arranges the medallions of lamb on the white dinner plates—one for the Captain, one for her boyfriend, one for me, one for her, adds a few tucks, sprinkles a whisper of parsley and rosemary on each portion, and flourishes the sides with ginger-grated cabbage and julienned potatoes. We nod to each other.

"Dinner!" she calls, and the men drag themselves away from work talk to size up the menu.

"That looks absolutely wonderful," compliments the Captain with a supportive smack of the lips. He escorts me to the table, smiling broadly, mirroring the giddy mood. His senior assistant smiles cautiously because we women aren't smiling—we are hiccuping back slurps of giggles.

"What have you girls been up to?" the senior assistant asks, tone mild, dark eyes suspicious.

"Let's eat," suggests the girlfriend. Linking her arm into his elbow, she leads him toward the table.

The Captain extends his hand to steer me to my seat, pulls my chair out gallantly, and waits until I organize myself before he sits down at the head of the table, a spot reserved especially for him.

We four are now seated, napkins folded in our laps, wineglasses raised in a toast, and wait for the host to begin. The senior assistant defers, nods to his boss, and respectfully requests the Captain start the meal.

"To the masterful chef, his lovely lady, I am honored by this most excellent dinner," eulogizes the Captain, "a dinner that we can eat before breaking down the set."

"*Bon appétit!*" The Captain clinks glasses all around.

"Cheers!" Everyone agrees.

The Captain cuts his meat with great delicacy.

We women are taking a great interest in his first bite. But raised with excellent table manners, the Captain lifts only a tiny morsel on his fork to his mouth.

Rave reviews.

We breathe out and start in on our plates. The men carry on with their conversation. We chew our tender lamb medallions daintily and hang on to their every word. The Captain cuts his meat again, another tiny slice from the very edge of the roast. The Captain chews politely. The conversation continues. Expectantly, eyes big, we girls raise our wineglasses to our lips.

The Captain cuts into his meat again, but it isn't going well. He looks down. He struggles with his knife. He ignores the tough cut, raises the fork to his mouth and continues with the conversation.

There is a dramatic pause.

Then a hushed, choking noise.

Forks midair, eyes on the Captain, we watch as he coughs into the linen napkin, then pulls a leggy cockroach from the folds of his napkin and places it to the side of the plate. His face turns chalky, but he doesn't say a word.

The senior assistant looks up from his meal to see why the sudden silence.

We girls can't hold our sides from splitting another moment and explode into hysterics.

It takes the Captain a few moments before he gets his bearings and slowly realizes this is a joke. When he sees the cockroaches are plastic, not real, he is caught. His upbringing demands him to be a good sport, but it's difficult because he would probably heave over the sides of the table if no one was looking.

His senior assistant doesn't give the cockroach a second thought except to check his own plate and remove a black plastic look-alike from the third slice in.

He shrugs, "Oh, she does that to me all the time. I'm always finding some little surprise inside my lunch box—nuts and bolts, dead mice, condoms."

The Captain nods sociably, but he never fully recovers his appetite, and the rest of the dinner, followed by his favorite liqueur and an authentic Cuban cigar, just doesn't taste the same.

At the end of the evening, the Captain and I kiss and hug the senior assistant and his art-director girlfriend good-bye, thank them for a tasty dinner, and wish them the best in their new locations. I know I am going to miss her.

I take the plastic cockroaches home with me and stockpile them deep in the ice tray in the freezer.

After a day, I forget about them.

The Captain doesn't.

THE LAST STRAW

CHRISTMAS AGAIN

We are five years into the relationship. I have just planted 350 tulip bulbs in the back of the barn at Thanksgiving, but have yet to see the results because it is the beginning of a New England winter; a raw green December's day that reminds me of a frozen sugar peapod that goes snap with one bite.

We have been fighting since Thanksgiving, which moves quickly into Christmas. Fighting becomes a holiday tradition. I don't even know why. Every year I hope we can get it right. Every year I always do something wrong. Holidays are neither of our strong points, and I wish we could erase this time of year and fast-forward to spring. Sometimes I think the Captain suffers from an onset of winter blues and needs a good dose of sunshine. Other times I think he just needs to stop pouring rum and tonics.

Even though the Captain is giving me the warning signals of an imminent breakdown by unreasonable outbursts of temper I can never predict, I am not paying attention to the meaning behind the lyrics.

The evening after my family leaves from a command Thanksgiving dinner cooked to perfection by the Captain himself, he calls me selfish because I draw the bathwater too hot for him to join in and storms out of the house. That same sunny morning, I am caught pulling the blinds up in the bathroom when he wants them down and knotted in a certain way. Sometimes it's the simple things I do that I can't get right—like stirring the pasta while it's cooking. Or pouring coffee for him too soon in the morning. Or turning the heat up one degree when the guests are sitting shoeless and shivering on the couch. Or stoking the woodstove when it needs attention. Or washing his dirty laundry with mine.

I never think to stop all the raging about by asking one simple question: *What's really the matter? What's wrong here?*

Instead, I tug on his arm and pull him upstairs, and we make love and the tension eases for a moment.

But the performances are very soon going to end with a two-year intermission. Only first, we have one last dinner together deep in the foggy stew of an almost January Provincetown.

NIGHT AT THE OPERA

PROVINCETOWN

We are driving out to Provincetown for a quick bite. A few nights ahead of New Year's Eve, this spontaneous dinner decision entails a foggy, damp, hour-long journey hurtling down the mid-Cape highway to its bitter end.

By the time we reach the twinkling lights at the tip of Race Point and find a restaurant open for dinner that keeps winter hours, we are cold, moody, very hungry, and irritable. We have only one choice; a dimly lit, waterfront establishment with hideous opera screeching out from behind a weathered red entrance door.

The Captain holds the door open; I move ahead, investigating the setting.

"It's okay," I review.

Inside it is a trendy place. We are lucky they will even seat us with only a forty-minute wait. The maître d' sniffs at our male and female combination and finally seats us in oblivion directly beneath a pair of Bang & Olufsen symphonic-quality speakers. At the long banquet table next to us, twenty men are outhustling each other, feting a new young preppy initiate into Provincetown society. Lots of leather, studs, sexual confusion. Lots of boy/boy trips to the bathroom.

When I go to freshen up, I am confronted with two bathroom doors, one labeled *"Us"*, one labeled *"Them"*. I am first amused, then confused. Then irritated with the psychological implications. I don't know which one to pick. But my urge is greater than my identity, and I squeeze around a giggling *"Them"* couple just emerging from the *"Us"* toilet and am hoping the toilet seat is down.

When I return to the table, I find our waitress hovering over my empty seat wearing only a two-pronged spiked leather brassiere and German-shepherd dog studs on her waist belt. High leather boots click the linoleum floor. Before I sit down, she eyes me from head to toe and ignores the Captain. This upsets him.

The opera-background ambience is knifing my ears with a high-pitched soprano aria from the death scene of *La Traviata*. Opera reminds me of deadly Saturday afternoons at home throughout my childhood because my father is a classical-music lover and listening to the matinee opera program on his new FM hi-fi becomes a household instrument of discord. My sisters and I learn to identify each recording, each soprano, each tenor, and each opera house. And learn to hate each of them equally.

I ask the waitress if they can turn the opera down, or preferably off.

She is annoyed, and says she doesn't think so, the owner loves opera.

I ask her to please check.

She disappears for two long choruses and finally returns to say, *"No, it's impossible."* Her tone is bitchier than mine. The request is denied with an eyebrow-lifting arrogance that makes me think we must be in France asking the concierge for an extra roll of toilet paper.

I resort to desperate measures.

I tell her my father is a famous opera singer who only just passed away two weeks ago. *"It's upsetting to hear this music. You understand,"* I explain.

The opera gets turned off.

The Captain gets pissed off.

Later that weekend, on New Year's Day, I get dropped off.

For two years.

BREAKUP #1

HAPPY NEW YEAR

ON THE PHONE

The Captain is a tit-for-tat guy.

I always believe handshakes mean fair play after the brawl. The Captain's nature is more biblical. He casts me out of the realm completely, closes the Garden of Eden gate right on my ankle, crippling any graceful exit. Only he does it by telephone.

Democratic on the outside, feudal on the inside, the Captain speaks but does not like being spoken to. Like Moses on Mt. Sinai, he throws the tablets down the mountain, striking me from the record. But I never find out exactly which commandments I break.

Even though he is not Jewish, he could be.

Christians are taught to turn the other cheek.

"*There will be blue cheese on the moon before we ever get back together!*" he shouts on one end of the phone.

"WRONG PLANET!" I shout back.

"*This is precisely the problem!*" he roars.

I slam the phone down.

He calls right back.

"*You'll never hang up on me again!*" He slams the phone down with finality.

Two silent weeks later I come home early from a depressing day of work and am shocked to confront all my worldly goods from the Cape house dumped on my blue-and-white checkerboard linoleum kitchen floor. Even my tired old toothbrush stuffed into a half-empty box of Tampax makes the cut. The final parting gesture—his set of my house keys dropped emphatically on the counter.

It is really over.

I dissolve into a fever of tears on the desecrated floor. His cruelty is shameless. My God, I think, *even the toothbrush.*

I want my daughter. I call the school.

She runs home and finds me still collapsed sobbing on the kitchen floor.

"He's hurt," she advises. "Why else would he do this?"

"Because he can."

"Call him up and yell at him." This is sage advice from an eight-year-old.

I call the studio and reach his assistant.

"*May I please speak with the Captain?*"

There is a muffled delay. But the Captain cannot resist the telephone.

"*What?*" His voice is cold.

"That was cruel." My tone echoes defeat.

"How else can I get you to listen!"

In the end, I go to bed. I read. I stare at the ceiling. I reconstruct the last three months, but I can't find the answer to the question I never asked. *What happened?* The stock market crashes but I don't care, I don't have any money to lose. The Desert Storm Gulf War is smoking up the seven-o'clock news with oil fires. I don't care. My house is heated by gas.

Eventually I get out of bed and take my daughter and run away to Tucson to my favorite ranch because it is my fortieth birthday. I search for the Native American Indian stuntman with the kachina fertility goddess. I find him again, but now he has a young, blond girlfriend and his magic is limited to himself. He gives me a charm-bracelet trinket, a souvenir silver feather in a small plastic box. And wishes me well.

When I come back home, I gather my reserves and throw a "nouveau poor" party to celebrate the recession and invite a hundred people I hardly know. The party is a success. Only not for me. The one person I want to show up, won't.

The Captain and I don't talk for two years, but somehow I know what is going on. I know when my work gets busy, his studio gets busier. I know when I buy a secondhand black trophy car, he buys a black turbocharged brand-new sports car. He hears I meet a nice guy photographer with a beautiful portfolio who is kind to me. I hear he is breakfasting with a never-married, no-children Cambridge ornithologist who likes herbal tea and my bathtub.

WHO CARES?

An editor writes and asks me the one question basic to any book development: *Who are you and why should the reader care about you?*

Again, good question. How do I answer this?

Why should the reader care about me when I struggle with his half-time caring for five years before Breakup #1, for two years while we are apart but not really parted, for another six years until I make my final leap to shore?

Why should the reader care about me when I'm so busy taking care of everybody else in my life, I don't have the sense to watch out for myself?

It is absolutely true I am hoping to get away with the barest minimum of digging deep into my own hope chest because I trust the smartness of the reader to understand I can be any woman, any woman in love with a one-foot-in, one-foot-out, man. I take that back. I'm not just any woman. I'm much more difficult.

If you know me, if I allow you to know me, would you like what you learn? Would you understand? Would you know I need a hug just about now? Or just one more line of encouragement to keep going—to keep writing?

Do you know that as tough as I might appear to those who collide with me briefly, what the hit party might not guess is that my heart breaks at the slightest dent—theirs and mine?

MISSING PARTS

I am in the recovery room. My head is pounding. The urge to retch penetrates the deep, pain-free unknowingness of general anesthesia and forces me into the here and now. An institutional-green, circular-draped curtain divides me from the other moans and cries. I listen as nurses' shoes, covered with operating room tissue paper, rustle back and forth beyond reach.

I am going to be sick.

I think I yelp, then move to sit up, but am absolutely paralyzed from the waist down. I see my stomach wrapped in white gauze oozing with sticky red blood. My arms are strapped to my sides, infusions of all kinds going into the crook of my elbow. Machines beep and whir. I cannot reach the panic button in time.

Before I am put under, the doctor warns me that the reaction to anesthesia is often worse than the operation. Now I know exactly what she means. I am dry-heaving and feel as if I am ripping open the seventy-five sutures barely holding my crosscut abdomen muscles and tissues together.

I'm sure this is it. I'm not going to make it to forty-one. Self-pity overwhelms me and mixes with the nausea. I'm feeling that the terror of being alone in the recovery room is deeper than the pain of losing a piece of my internal geography.

A nurse hears me, draws open the curtain, and lifts my head in the nick of time. She holds a curved plastic basin under my dry chapped lips and gives me the go-ahead. "You're okay," she says after the third round, and comforts me with a pat on the arm. I don't know about that. I don't feel okay. I feel like I am dead and have definitely not gone to the heaven side of things. I can't account for the time. I can't feel my legs. I need to vomit again. I try to breathe in and out and control the urge.

The nausea subsides somewhat.

"Your son is outside in the hall," she says. "He'd like to see you. He's been waiting for hours."

I don't know whom she is talking about. I don't have a son. I am sure she has me mixed up with some other patient. I'm a single mother of an eight-year-old daughter who should be waiting at home with the baby-sitter until my parents arrive to take over.

"Can I send him in? It's not usually allowed, but he is insisting."

The nurse wipes my mouth clean. I listen to her padding away. The truth is, I feel too awful to care about sorting out the identity of this mystery guest. I immediately forget about it.

The curtain parts gently again.

A very tall, lanky, boyish young man with thin, shoulder-length, strawberry-blond hair and a shiny stud in one ear stands awkwardly over the arm bars of the hospital bed and reaches for the only hand not taped down.

I am shocked to see the son of the man who is no longer my man.

Folding himself into the side chair, his son comes to sit with me. He comes to wait for me to recover from this major operation because it is not a minor affair. He comes because he knows I'm alone. He comes because his father is no longer in the relationship, because his father is now with a new woman. His son strokes my cheek with one sensitive long finger. He holds my hand and sits with me, allowing me to lie back against the pillow and feel safe to close my eyes.

I don't know how long he stays holding my hand. I feel guilty for eating up his evening and eventually wave him away. But the nurse is not wrong. There is no mistake. The confusion is my own. Of his father's five sons from the first marriage, all now quite grown, he is the youngest, but the closest to me.

He shows up like a son.

And I am lying there still wishing to death for his father.

MY BED

It is the second winter without the Captain. Even though I am seeing someone else, it is not the same. My heart is not in it. The only place I want to be is in my own bed, alone.

The weather is miserable, a slushy, raw, wet February. Every evening slogging home from work, I glance wistfully at a cherry-wood four-poster Shaker bed dressing up a furniture storefront window on my street corner. I think perhaps the new bed will help cheer me up, erase a few ghosts. Guilt, treason and economics, however, carry more weight. I want this bed, but can't justify the purchase.

I consult my dear friend, an elderly French *vicomte,* who is forced from the comforts of his own feather-bed chamber in his ancestral Loire Valley château when he is exiled to the States during the Second World War. One Sunday afternoon, I take him window-shopping for advice and he doesn't disappoint me.

He taps his gold-knobbed walking stick on the icy sidewalk below the store window and shifts his winterized beret over a dramatic pair of bushy white eyebrows.

"*Now, that is a bed!*" he collaborates. "By all means! Absolutely!"

I march right in and hand the salesperson my credit card.

The bed is delivered within the week.

I retreat into its magnificent four-poster shoulders and wait . . .

AWARD NIGHT

. . . until September.

It is Scratch Award night, the Oscars of commercial film advertising.

I never go to this particular affair. Or rather, I haven't gone, certainly not willingly, in the last five years. If I do, I know I will squirm among the crowd of polished self-congratulating agency account executives or slink to the back of the auditorium, invisible amid a crush of black-dressed art directors cynically focused on the parade of who's hot and who's not.

But this year my front is braver. My ten-year-old daughter is delighted to be attending with me. She should be. A fifteen-second commercial spot featuring a devil with syringes for horns she creates for her school's "Just Say No to Drugs" ad contest is playing center stage in the lobby video monitor. No one knows it's a ten-year-old's handiwork or that I have secretly submitted her entry in the name of our agency. Not even the judges.

The truth is, I would be happier to be home in bed. But my daughter won't hear of it.

"It's my very own video!" she cockadoodle-doos. "We just *have* to go. Maybe it will win Best of Show!"

I look at her skeptically. She hasn't learned about the heart-break of psoriasis yet.

"The tickets cost fifty dollars each," I inform her.

"You never pay for them anyway," she reminds me.

We go.

I drag my daughter up to the balcony, acknowledge several arty colleagues dressed in black, kiss two or three cheeks, and find a pair of seats surrounded by the goodwill of a few faithful media friends and former agency associates.

"Hey, how the hell are you?" An old buddy art-director friend I haven't seen in a couple of years leans over from the row behind to catch my ear. *"Oh, and by the way, I just saw your ex,"* he whispers with a conspiratorial pause. "He's downstairs."

"The Captain?" I stutter.

"The very one."

"But he never comes to these things," I argue.

"He's right down there." His voice is sure.

"With someone?" I pursue.

"I didn't see anyone."

"Alone?"

"It looks that way."

My daughter nods. "I told you, Mommy."

I'm glad the theater is dark. My face is red. I can feel the light beaming directly off the dome of the Captain's head from the orchestra seat right up into the balcony, performing laser surgery on my heart.

I argue with myself. I won't go look for him. I will go. I won't. This must be fate. There's no such thing as fate. There is a reason for this. It's a random act. God is telling me something. My daughter is telling me something.

"Do it, Mommy, you know you want to."

I do.

I squeeze my daughter's hand and entrust her to the care of my art-director friend. "I'll be right back," I whisper.

Making my way up the narrow balcony aisle, I fumble for the exit, wind my way two flights down the red carpet stairway, push against a black door, and find myself in the main lobby, inhabited by only a few tuxedoed stragglers smoking in the corners.

The unattended double doors to the main orchestra section stand like an open invitation. Deep inside, a screen projecting award-winning commercials dominates the darkness. The place is packed with hundreds of heads all looking forward. The identification task seems daunting. Long-haired heads. Short-haired heads. Male heads. Female heads.

Balding heads.

One particular balding head with gray hair bobs higher than the rest over the horizon of chairs like a lighthouse beacon.

I grope down the center aisle, making my way toward the one empty seat left that appears to glow in the dark in the theater.

"*Is this seat taken?*" I whisper when I reach the right row.

The Captain blinks up at me in wonder.

"*No. It's free.*" He covers his shy surprise. With a gracious movement, he shifts his jacket over one seat to accommodate me. His pleased face is warm, his smile like home.

I slip right into place.

"*How the hell are you?*" I whisper with a familiar intimacy.

And he tells me.

He tells me his brother dies only two weeks ago. His father is fading. He is no longer with the Cambridge ornithologist. He looks sad and lost. I tell him my daughter is sitting upstairs in the balcony and that I am sure she would like to see him. I tell him about her exhibited entry. He grins.

"Let's go up, I want to see her," he says.

The Captain hovers about us the rest of the evening. My daughter does not win Best of Show, but she is still proud and holds court for a few more minutes by the monitor playing her reel of art.

When the show ends, the Captain offers to get our coats from the hatcheck girl. "I'll meet you at the bottom of the stairs and walk you out," he says like old times.

My daughter skips light of foot down the red-carpeted steps behind him.

I am suddenly shy. I am wondering if my slip is showing. Or if my skirt is twisted. I take one step down, then another. The staircase looks infinite. The Captain is now staring up at me from the bottom of the stairs. His eyes dance on mine. I feel the pressure mounting.

I check my skirt but not my footing and catch my heel in the carpet.

I trip.

I skid two steps at a time and land flat on my backside.

My daughter looks up the staircase at me in horror.

The Captain sighs and shakes his head.

I pick myself up and pretend it hasn't happened.

But it has.

The faux pas is made. The cheese is still blue on the moon.

The Captain, my daughter, and I walk outside together in an uncomfortable silence. At the curb, the Captain kisses me a light good-bye on my cheek and gives my daughter a solid hug. When we get to the corner, the urge to grab him and ask him to come home with us is almost too great to bear.

"Come over," I ask, but I already know the answer.

He shakes his head. *"I'll call you sometime,"* he says. Then, as the light turns green, he waves and turns right.

We turn left.

Holding hands, my daughter and I trudge back to our car and go home, prizeless.

BACK TOGETHER AGAIN

THE CALLBACK

I trip forward.

Two months after Scratch Night, I wake up one morning and feel free. I stop dreaming of him, stop missing him, clear out my top drawer, wave the staircase humiliation away, and with one sweeping gesture, release the interim boyfriend from any further obligation. It is holiday season once again. I am alone. And I don't care. After two years of free-falling, both feet have landed on the ground. Jumping through Thanksgiving without a stumble, I understand the very act of letting go has increased my stretch.

I can live without the Captain.

My daughter congratulates me. *"Finally."* She sighs.

The phone rings late one weekday night.

"Hi," he says.

"Who's this?" I ask, not connecting the voice immediately.

"It's me." His voice sounds indignant. "The Captain."

"Oh, sorry."

"I told you I'd call. I've been away until now."

I do not ask him where he's been.

"Have dinner with me a week from Thursday?" The sureness of his invitation wavers at the question mark.

"Hmm," I answer slowly. "I don't think so."

"Why not?"

"I'll be out of town."

"Really? Where are you going?" The casual question posed ever so lightly sounds insistent.

"Chicago. Client presentation."

"Then how about this Friday?"

"That won't work."

"Why not?"

"I'm leaving Friday night for California."

"I thought you said you're going to Chicago?"

"I am, next week. This weekend I'm flying to California."

There is a pause.

"When do you get back?"

"It's a busy month.

"With what?" His curiosity skips a beat.

"With my daughter and the holidays."

"How's she doing?"

"Fine," I acknowledge. "But she is still turning men away at the door."

"How's that?"

"She asked the last guy who came for dinner if he ever considered joining Hair Club for Men."

There is relief in his short laugh. *"That's my girl!"*

"Look, why don't I call you after the holidays?" I offer. "Maybe we could do dinner sometime in January. I've got to run."

"Call me," he says, "when you get back."

ROAST BEAST

A month later he calls me again.

"How about dinner at the studio on Thursday?" he invites. "I'll cook."

I don't remember when we finally sit down and eat. I don't remember exactly what we talk about. I remember only that images of my art-directed work still hang on his studio walls. The dinner plates are still the white ones with the black rim I helped choose years ago. The black linen napkins are pulled through the onyx-black rings I find for a past Thanksgiving feast. My daughter's crayon drawings still dangle from a piece of Scotch tape on the white-painted brick walls.

Even though two years have passed, nothing has changed.

Dinner is the same: roast beef, broccoli with hollandaise sauce, rice pilaf.

But I especially remember dessert.

We are sitting on opposite sides of the studio kitchen waiting for the coffee to perk. I am reclining over two kitchen chairs. The Captain stretches comfortably out on the gray industrial-carpeted floor.

We have eaten a heavy meal. The bottle of Merlot is nearly empty.

But the Captain still looks hungry.

I am starving.

"Why are you over there on the floor and I am here on the chair?" I ask. "Don't you think this is ridiculous?"

He does.

BACK TO BED

THE CAPE

There have been just a few little changes while I've been away.

On my first overnight back in the Cape house, I am confused to find an unfamiliar but beautifully handcrafted Santa Fe–style bed of deep cherry wood with twin matching night tables filling what was once the Captain's spartan master bedroom space. I only remember a simple unframed queen mattress and springs on a metal frame.

My amazement at the coincidence of the new cherry-wood bed that looks almost like my new cherry-wood bed doesn't count. I am hurt he would even think to get a new bed while he is with the in-between girlfriend.

"How could you!" I accuse.

"But I really built this bed for you," he whispers as he leads me toward the covers. "I measured it exactly to fit the two of us."

"*While you were with her?*" My voice is skeptical.

"I couldn't get you out of my mind."

I believe him.

We make love with the relief of old lovers unbuttoning a too tight waistband. It feels heavenly.

"But this isn't my side of the bed," I murmur, slightly disoriented when he rolls me over to the opposite pillow into a sleeping position.

My observation gets ignored.

"*This isn't my side of the bed,*" I insist and jump out of bed. "You switched sides!"

"Don't be ridiculous," says the Captain.

"I can't sleep on this side," I argue.

"Yes, you can. You always do." But he avoids my eyes by picking up a financial newsletter off the nearby new night table. "Stop making a fuss. Come to bed."

He's right and he's wrong.

At my house I always sleep on the outside of the bed, the left side, because it's easier to get to the bathroom rather than crawl over him during the night. At the Cape, I always sleep on the right side because of the reading lamp.

The switch disturbs me, but that's not the only thing.

The sheets are flannel, cream-colored. I don't know them. The bed is spread with a Mexican Aztec quilt cover I also don't know. There is a scent to the sheets that is not mine.

"I can't sleep on these," I tell him, my arms folded under my chest as I stand by the edge of the bed.

"Get in," he says, looking over his half glasses at me. He coaxes me with a boyish smile.

"Not until we change the sheets."

"There is nothing the matter with these sheets."

"Someone else has been sleeping on these sheets."

"Come to bed. It's late."

"Then change the sheets first."

"It's all in your head," he says. "We are not changing the sheets now."

"Then I'll sleep in the guest room."

"No, you won't." He gets testy.

We don't change the sheets.

I don't sleep in the guest room.

I don't sleep, period.

I lie awake the entire night because the herbal scent I can't exactly define disturbs the very air I breathe in on this wrong side of the bed.

The sheets and pillowcases get washed the next morning.

I want to throw them right out. Instead, they remain on the bed for the next six winters. But I never really get used to them.

And seven years later I find out the in-between girlfriend is never really quite gone.

BEST BUDDY

For-ty years on, when a - far and a-sun-der Par-ted

p

hen you look back, and for - get - ful-ly won-der What you were

hen, it may be, there will of - ten come o'er you, Glimp-ses of n

SCRABBLE

Time does funny things to relationships. We are loving and fighting on and off for the next six years. And the magic never goes away for me. For his birthday, the last January of our lives together, I give him a magnetic poetry kit with French words because he is trying so hard to learn the language. That night, sleepless, I find myself downstairs in the cold kitchen at three A.M. moving the magnetic word tiles around and around the door of the refrigerator, creating a love poem in French for him to find in the morning.

Sometimes, though, as I slide through my forties, I get the sense he likes only the feel of me, not the look of me. There are no snapshots of us as a couple hanging in the Cape house alongside photographs of his five sons and one new daughter-in-law.

Nor pictures of me or my growing-up daughter, even though he makes movies for a living. I freeze in front of a camera. So maybe that's it. I don't know. Once a visiting friend catches a shot of the two of us, arm in arm, and sends us a copy. I like it and keep it in his kitchen until one day it's gone from the counter.

And then when I think I might finally have the Captain's attention, when we are almost free of the responsibilities of my child rearing and his work ambitions, Best Buddy doesn't make it to admiral and gets kicked into early retirement from the navy. He and the Captain are both only in their midfifties when this happens.

Best Buddy, out of touch for ten years, is now in need of someone to play with. He sends the Captain an SOS in the form of a retirement celebration invitation.

I am not included.

That's when the real trouble begins.

The Captain goes down to Best Buddy's last-call retirement party in North Carolina. After he comes back, he decides to go sailing for the rest of his life.

And mine.

I quickly learn Best Buddy cannot be ignored. His vision of the Captain's early retirement is drawn and quartered into a powerful master scheme. This includes persistent nagging about planning for the future whether it's one hour or ten years away. Best Buddy's specialties are: money, trust funds, retirement plans, old-age homes, scrimping, saving, living off government pensions, making long-term investments, buying the right stocks, and hoarding the right bonds. He is also a champion of accepting other people's invitations to help crew on their boats as a money saving way of getting from here to there on someone else's diesel fumes. It doesn't take me long to understand that all he has to do is provide the wind.

So when Best Buddy gets hold of my Captain's ear and starts chewing, he bites right through to the inner drum. Like a child with a chronic infection, the Captain grows deaf to any other point of view, especially mine.

BEST BUDDY

Can a triangle have four sides?

I hear about Best Buddy for years. He and the Captain start their youth together as roommates in Hastings-on-the-Thames, an elite boarding school in England for the crust that is a tad less upper than the royalty who attend Eton. The loyalty at this school is fierce and the old-boy network is very old. The two boys are educated in straw-boater-hat tradition during the era of white gloves and large garden-party hats. The Captain's father, posted to highly visible Embassy Row, London, agrees that a British boarding school offers a great social advantage. *"Children should neither be seen nor heard,"* he remarks. At the same time Best Buddy's expatriate American father is living the life of a dabbling portrait painter in château country in the Loire Valley with his brood of four plus wife with a trust fund. Because France is not the proper training ground for a son of the American Revolution, Best Buddy Sr. also sends his son to Hastings for a stiff-upper-lip education.

How-Kind-of-You-to-Let-Me-Come is the rule of thumb at Hastings.

The Captain understands this and saves Best Buddy Jr. from being a complete outcast. He looks out for him and includes him in his charmed circle. Best Buddy is the Captain's best and most loyal friend, and he should be. The Captain snips him through the school hazing initiations, shades him in his sports' spotlight, steps him through the social whirl. Best Buddy is probably a better student than the Captain, but like a dislocated shoulder, he wears his social desperation higher on his sleeve.

At Hastings, the Captain is the most popular boy. He is handsome, an athlete, a rugby captain, a star. Even a school monitor. As a most favored roommate, Best Buddy enjoys being the toad to the Captain's prince.

In fact, Best Buddy talks of nothing else than the days he shoeshines at Hastings.

Like I say, Best Buddy shows up in our relationship when the navy early retires him, possibly because they fear if he becomes admiral, everyone will have to sit up and listen to him.

Instead, I have to listen to him.

Puffed up, red in the face, and sealed with a salty outer layer of seasoned fat like a baked Virginia ham on Thanksgiving, Best Buddy can give you stage-III hypertension. He enjoys poking all women, especially me, with endless pontifications, judgments, character critiques, and woman bashing.

Before I meet him, I imagine a fit, tall, distinguished, handsome, Annapolis-type officer in a crisp white uniform; gallant, charming, sophisticated, worldly; a strong, morally upright naval commander.

Instead, I find a midsized, jowly, gray-haired, less-than-fit military retiree, desperately trying to hold on to the traditional trappings of his blue-blood, Social Register American heritage. It's a little awkward, because Best Buddy has four fingers on his left hand. He loses his signet-ring pinkie one late afternoon early in his marriage when the sudden tug of his fishing line catches around the rotating propellers of his outboard motor. But that doesn't keep Best Buddy from climbing. Despite being born only to a memory of a manor, he's proud of his white-bread-and-mayonnaise culture. He honors the Puritan ethic by wearing the same food-stained white polo shirt three days in a row, along with Scotch-and-soda-spotted khaki pants and a worn, canvas blue belt with little white whales, stretched to its limit because one of everything is enough. And besides, changing clothes is for girls.

As he loves to remind me, *"There are no women in duck blinds."*

I am supposed to be offended.

Although I hear about Best Buddy for years, I only meet him and his stalwart wife after the Captain and I recover from Breakup #1. In fairness, Best Buddy has no idea I exist. Or existed. The Captain never thinks to tell him. Or I am not important enough or presentable enough to show off. When we finally meet, Best Buddy cannot get used to me. Or my uppity feminist ways. He is determined to get me permanently fired, and is surely sorry he isn't around for consultation when I am rehired after Round #1.

Now on land after thirty-five years as a United States naval officer, Best Buddy sees himself as a gentleman farmer. He and his wife buy a rural, waterlogged plot up a creek of the Dismal Swamp in a part of North Carolina that is somewhere between redneck and Uncle Tom's cabin with a new addition. There are a few rolling hills here, a sprinkle of old glory plantations with slave quarters intact, some dripping Spanish moss, and a hint of sterling-silver trays on sideboards slippery with wet mint juleps.

But a few nautical miles inland, the atmosphere turns into New Hampshire trailer park south of the Mason-Dixon Line. The area is not stingy with the backwoods props. There is a complete sprawl of fire-hazard country-western dives, greasy Fat Girl Diners, "po'boys" at the local luncheonette, stuck-in-second-gear third-generation station wagons. Best Buddy's favorite toy is an old red tractor that works every other Monday, an American icon that has also been put out to pasture.

A retirement community of midranked military types populates the terrain. Most are navy, with a few air-force personnel sprinkled in because the land is cheap, the housing large, the heating bills negligible, and the pensions can cover the short money for membership in the local yacht club.

There is a lot of drinking going on down here. A lot of parties, socials at the yacht club, pig roasts, gossip, a place where almost anyone can feel superior just by putting on a blue blazer.

Food at SpinCup, the Southern supermarket chain, is cheap. Beer is cheap. Gas is cheap. Talk is cheap, and Best Buddy likes to get his money's worth. Considering his affection for thrift, he flaps his lips frequently. The only talk Best Buddy passes on is psychobabble, which he disdains as women's work. But he's good at dropping names. He can't help himself. He is dying for someone to drop his name.

I will happily accommodate.

The truth is, on a good day, before the drinking begins, I like Best Buddy. He is funnier than he thinks. He is also an excellent sailor and makes docking, anchoring, cooking on board, fixing broken bits and pieces look easy and effortless. The tension is not climaxing from his brow. He is not exactly persnickety, although I can think of a lot of P words that he is. He is hardly personally fastidious, although Best Buddy keeps his own sister boat shipshape, and he sails her comfortably, ruling his roost with certain laws and regulations you just have to live by.

I have to respect the guy even though it hurts. Best Buddy's job in the navy as commander of nuclear ships means he can park them in any tight berth just by barking orders and being obeyed. Best Buddy is used to being obeyed in the navy, where he has his rank to back him up. Home is a different story. He thinks he is king of his manor, but because he likes to use the expression *"Off with her head!"* a little too freely when he discusses me with the Captain, I sometimes think he is the queen.

It is too easy to make fun of Best Buddy. He takes himself too seriously, and that's what's so ridiculous. He is his own caricature of all that is found in a pedigreed WASP, twenty generations less successful than his original *Mayflower* forefather. Although his family name has fallen on rustier times, he, Best Buddy, is determined to drag it back up the front hallway stairs and nail the signature distinctively under the gilt-edged, framed portrait of his bygone ancestor.

Sometimes I feel tender about all his relentless efforts. I wonder if he knows, deep inside his polo shirt, he is trading off the family name like a baseball-card collector with a pack no one values anymore.

SEASPEAK

AT SEA

I have never been at a loss for words.

I speak English because I'm lucky to come out headfirst and get delivered in the United States. Hebrew, because I learn to stand on my own two feet in Israel. Other languages I pick up along the way: useful police-station French, a smattering of Dutch. I can even have a baby in basic Afrikaans, which I do, and end up in South Africa with a strong daughter I name after a very fine ironwood walking stick. Last year, I grab a few words of Arabic while working in Amman and can now move across the Jordanian border quicker than a terrorist. Even a long-ago teaching stint in a high school near Hiroshima teaches me how to tell the Japanese I don't speak Japanese in Japanese, and then to bow and ask their forgiveness. I think I am pretty language-friendly for an American. I have a good ear. I can mimic an accent and take it on as my own after listening to the first dangling participle out of the mouth of an immigrant Eritrean cabdriver asking me for directions home from Logan Airport.

Or maybe I just don't have my own personality.

When it comes to the language of sailing, however, I'm a tongue-tied illiterate.

It is thirteen boat years later, and I still can't tell *port* from *starboard*. Someone gives me a tip once that helps: port = left = four letters. Therefore, starboard = right. Left and right, that's easy. I ask the Captain why I can't just say left and right? He answers with another question. "That's fine, only which direction are you facing on the boat?"

Good question. *Which direction am I facing?*

Now it gets complicated.

I can be on the right side of the boat but also be on the wrong side of the Captain. It depends, you see, on the direction of the *bow* (the tits-forward front of the ship reserved for mermaids) and the *stern* (the tail end, where the U.S. flag waves in the wind above the diesel fumes to let the Coast Guard know this is not a hostile vessel).

I always feel a little affected when I use boatspeak. It takes me forever to break down and call the bathroom the *head,* the lead line that ties the dinghy to the boat the *painter*. I keep looking for a smock and a palette. I finally learn that a rope line is a *sheet*, a sheet is not a *sail,* the mainsail is not the *jib,* the jib is not the *spinnaker*. A *fender* is not on a car but is stowed in a boat locker in the cockpit and looks like a giant sausage stuffed into a nautical blue nylon casing. Six fenders are access-ready so they can be quickly tied against the outer hull of the sailboat to cushion the blow on the good chance the boat should ram into the fuel dock. They are also used to prevent scraping the hull paint off the sides when the yacht-club launch arrives, or when Best Buddy decides to raft his sailboat up to us for the night to save on slip fees.

A *slip* is not what is showing under a dress, but is a drive-in parking slot the boat slips into to get more comfortable at night. A slip means bringing the boat into a full-service marina where a narrow berth waits to safely cradle the boat for a few days or a week, allowing the mutinying crew to jump ship directly onto the dock without having to row ashore. At a slip, there's usually a laundry, a grocery, his-and-her hot showers with electrical outlets, a place to trade in very used paperbacks, and a ship-like Store-24 where the Captain spends his stock dividends on useful items to keep the boat shipshape.

Staying overnight at a slip eats away at the small change in the Captain's Tupperware container over the ice chest. A slip is expensive because the marina charges by the foot, which means the marina charges by how long the boat is, how many feet she is below the belt. This is a very sensitive issue. The Captain's boat, an elegant sloop with very fine lines, is 36 feet long, and draws 5 feet below the keel. Best Buddy's sailboat is 34 feet, draws 3.5 feet below the keel, but is broader at the beam. The conclusions are obvious. I'd like to say that the guy with the bigger boat wins, but this is not always true.

Good sailors test their skills pulling into a slip—it's tight and tricky. And when there's a screwup, well, the rabbit dies. If the Captain misses the ease of the turn, or shoots in too soon, he has to back up, try again, or risk an accident. Every captain on every boat filling the other 250 slips watches the performance. My Captain is acutely aware of the public. If there is trouble, it's usually because I'm not paying careful attention, or throw the bowline short of its mark, or can't read his mind about which end is up.

If we don't go into a slip, we can pick up a yacht-club or town *mooring,* a mushroom-cap buoy I always miss catching the first time around with the telescope-extending boat hook. This also costs money, but is generally less expensive than a slip. The mooring is an important piece of property. Professionally installed by a hired diver, a mooring is always there before you are. A mooring ties the yacht to an assigned space, usually in a crowded harbor, and not only keeps the boat from slamming into other moored boats, but saves the Captain the anxiety of dragging his anchor through a sand bed for the rest of the night. In short, a mooring is similar in methodology and security to chaining an expensive ten speed bicycle to a parking lot meter.

Or we can *anchor* outside the city limits in the free harbor. I like the privacy afforded by anchoring. I don't like the work because the Captain has to do most of it. The anchor gets *dropped* when we stop and *weighed* when we leave. There is no scale, here, although pulling the anchor chain down below into its home in the hold at the foot of the bunk bed is a heavy, nasty job, which I get elected to do because I am small and can fit into the crawl space and yank. This is where the expression *yanking the chain* gets its workout. I learn to put rubber gloves on to save my hands and fingernails because the 150 feet of chain links are filled with oozing ocean excrement, brackish river sludge, briny tangled seaweed, and razor-sharp barnacles. Best Buddy throws his head back and laughs at me when he sees me pull on the rubber gloves. But I must be onto something, because the next day I see his wife on her knees, yanking their chain through the hold opening like a midwife tugging on the birth cord, and her hands are deep in yellow rubber.

And now it's time to come about.

Coming about is not what happens as a result of sex, but relates to changing the sailing tack to work with the fluky wind that might shift from north to south or east to west or vice versa at any given whim. An alternating wind means altering the navigational course. This minute-by-minute decision creates a sudden lurch to the side, which means I must physically shift my curled-up-with-a-book reading position from a comfortable port to an uncomfortable starboard, or from a comfortable starboard to an uncomfortable port. Coming about comes about when the mainsail *boom* swings over the cockpit. I know I'm supposed to bob down to avoid the driving boom or get punched in the head (not the bathroom head). The Captain issues a warning before changing sailing directions: *"Ready about!"* he shouts, *"Hard a-lee!"* These words are spoken out loud like a cult chant even when I'm not there and the only passenger on board is a seagull. I never quite get the meaning of *"hard a-lee."* *"Heartily?"* *"Hard as Lee?"* *"Hardly?"* But I know I have to hurry and turn the wheel in one of two directions, port or starboard, then duck down to avoid the boom, or die.

Because the Captain is a stickler for old English, and Best Buddy is an absolute fanatic for proper sailing terms, I don't muck around with the words. And anyway, when the two of them are sailing together and I also happen to be on board, they are so busy gabbing between themselves about sailing details, I usually get the silent treatment.

The fact is, I grow stupid on the boat. Over the years I lose my verbal skills, my bearings, my grip, my memory, my energy, my sense of self. I am trying to be first mate to his second career at sea, but because I am only the girlfriend, not a wife, I don't even know what to call myself.

NIGHT OF THE
BARBED WIRE

We are moored at a yacht club in Essex. A snooty one. A 1930s three-story, airy-summer-cottage kind that has old worn Cape shingles with a rambling veranda roping it off from the harbor. The name escapes me, maybe because it's too exclusive to remember. Even the rest rooms make me feel like an interloper. A curved-leg mahogany table nestles between camp-style toilet stalls and a plastic molded one-piece shower with a throwaway paper mat, the kind you find in motel bathrooms. On the table sits a blue clothbound yacht-club membership book. The list of Cape Ann society is engraved in alphabetical order on pages and pages of Crane's creamy white paper. I flip through the book and notice quite a few double-digit names that sound like the Captain's and think perhaps sailing is a genetic disorder.

We are having dinner at the yacht club. Two hoots on the horn, the launch arrives, steered capably by a tanned yacht boy wearing a blue polo shirt (Ralph Lauren), khaki pants (The Gap), and boat shoes (Timberland). It is always a performance; the getting off the boat, getting on the launch, dragging the canvas tote bag stuffed with towels, shower goods, and clean clothes.

He says after our showers he will wait for me in the harbor-side porch bar. We part on the staircase. I go one floor below to the women's shower room. I am thrilled to wash my hair under a rush of endless hot water and I take my time. I finally step out into the steamy damp room, then pull out my traveling hair dryer because there is electricity and an outlet. It takes me longer than necessary—to wash, towel-dry, put on makeup, dress, dry my hair. At the vanity, I am getting dirty side looks from pink-sweatered ladies who are at the club to dine, not to bathe, and have only descended to the bathroom to wash their hands before martinis.

Streaking a final touch of lipstick on my mouth, I take a last look in the mirror, wishing I was younger, thinner, or invisible, then scramble up the creaking wooden staircase to the English oak-paneled dining room. The Captain is still waiting for me on a wicker chair at the edge of the porch, blue blazer in place unbuttoned over a slightly crumpled blue-and-white pin-striped shirt, gray cotton boat slacks with multipockets, keys dangling from belt loop, legs crossed at the knee, sea-beaten boat shoes with half-tied laces slipped over tanned, sockless feet. With his signature captain's beard, he looks like an advertisement for sailing. Or private banking.

As I navigate the foyer, I bump into a boat-shoed, sunny staff waitress on her way into the dining room shouldering a heavy platter of boiled Maine lobsters, Ipswich fried clams, and coleslaw. I mumble "sorry" to her and think awful thoughts: some privileged member's perfect college daughter's character-building summer job.

"No problem," she answers cheerily.

She points to the handsome older man in the wicker chair. He is holding a drink.

"Are you looking for him?"

I nod.

She flashes an I-thought-so smile and whispers conspiratorially, *"He says he's waiting for the love of his life."*

I look at her, confused. "Who's that?"

Honestly, I don't even associate myself with the line.

I know what she is thinking. She is thinking how lucky can a girl be to have such a devoted man, still in love at his age. She takes it for granted he's a sailor. I know she is thinking exactly what he intends her to think.

So why can't I accept such an outrageous possibility, that I, in fact, am the love of his life?

Here's why:

Because later, much later, after a semireasonable meal and one bottle of Merlot at yacht-club insider's prices, we launch back to the boat. It is very dark but the boat's anchor lights are illuminated, and the launch boy deftly pulls up port to starboard.

The Captain quickly pushes me forward.

I am to hop from the motoring launch over the safety lines of our boat and get myself into the cockpit. Gracefully. The launch putters, stutters; my one leg is halfway over the side, the other leg is balancing between launch and our ship by my bare-legged inner thigh. I am not ready for the final leap over the wire lines. They are too high for me. I am too short-legged for them. I have begged him many times to unhook an opening in the safety lines so I can leap on board in safe passage, but open lines are not a sign of good seamanship. Instead, I stumble, miss a beat, yell against the wind that I need one more second to get my footing. He shouts back, voice angry. He orders me to get off the launch "*immediately*." He pushes the launch back off from kissing the sloop's hull, and I press my bare thigh deep into the wire cable and propel myself, ready or not, over the lines. The wire rung bites deeply into my inner-thigh flesh and snaps back again against my skin. Tears of raw pain blur my vision as I skid inelegantly over the wires into the cockpit.

I am furious that the launch boy and the exit performance are more important than I am. I shout at him. He ignores my pain, waves the launch away, pushes open the hatch, ducks down the companionway, first stowing the tote bag and his wallet in their proper compartments, and pours himself a nightcap, livid face and white beard steaming with indignity.

The next morning, a deep, cruel purple-and-red bruise the size of a cast-iron skillet stains the inside length of my thigh, the color so garishly vermilion it startles the eye. "I told you I hurt myself," I say. He harrumphs. After all, when he slices his size twelve foot through to his toe in the middle of the Caribbean, spurting more blood than is healthy, he says nothing to the crew. Instead he sews up the five-inch gash by himself with a net needle and fishing line, and limps through the rest of the trip, waving away questions about why he can't get his swollen foot into his shoe.

Let's be fair. The Captain doesn't treat the injured any more deferentially than he treats himself. On a boat there are always the walking wounded: the seasick, the insect-bite infections, finger slices, sunstroke, anchor-chain catches, stomachaches, dehydration, torn shoulder muscles, and so on; but nothing is serious as long as the Captain can still pour a drink at sundown.

He, however, has an incredible knack of making everything hard, harder.

And I have an incredible knack of fighting him every inch of the way.

WORK ECONOMICS

مديرية الأمن العام / ادارة الاقامة والحدود

يسمح له بالاقامة

Entrée / Entrées   *Visas*   *Departure / Sorties*

اعتبار من ١٩٩٨/٢/٢١

ولغايه ١٩٩٨/٢/٢١

الرقم المتسلسل ٢٨١٦٢

التاريخ ١٩٩٨/٢/٢٦

مدير ادارة الاقامة والحدود

May 31 99

المملكة الأردنية الهاشمية
THE HASHEMITE KINGDOM OF JORDAN

11 - APR 1998

DEPARTURE

المملكة الأردنية الهاشمية
THE HASHEMITE KINGDOM OF JORDAN

PENALTY CLAUSE

THE CORNER OFFICE

In between sailing and seething, I am also working for a living.

This fact of life doesn't go away as I mature. I am counting down the years until my daughter becomes a contributing financial servant, and I am counting on the Captain to help me retire with grace and security.

I don't count on trouble.

I don't count, period.

The Captain says that I set everything up and fling it into motion so what happens happens without me having to bear any responsibility for the lop of the boomerang which always smacks me in the head. *Always.*

For example:

After years of hoofing it around the United States and sometimes Europe, with oversized portfolios, which don't fit in the overhead compartment, for the clients of my company, I get bored and my computer arm hurts. How many hip new corporate identity programs can I get excited about designing and convincing clients to buy? I am looking for a way out, a new challenge.

I'm working on this pitch:

Everyone in my department takes three months maternity leave when there's a baby to be had. After fifteen years raising the infant design group into a mature, moneymaking adult, along with single-handedly raising my daughter during this entire period without leave, maternity or other, I want to have a sabbatical, too.

By divine providence or sheer coincidence, I get myself invited by the Queen of Jordan to work on a three-month project helping Palestinian refugee women create ethnic textile products to market for export. It's an offer I don't want to refuse.

The method of my own self-exile comes about in a very messy way.

My sister-close colleague at the advertising agency finds a fax from Jordan delivered and left on my office desk chair confirming the invitation before I have a chance to discuss the sabbatical with her, before I even see the fax. I am not expecting to hear from the Jordan project with such speed. Nothing ever moves quickly in the Middle East, so I don't even bother her about my possible invitation because it is not confirmed and might never be confirmed and I don't want to upset her until I have to. And, well, because I hate the conflicts I create.

But she gets to my chair before I do. She reads the fax because she can't ignore the glare of the Royal Court of Jordan seal across the masthead. She is furious, feels betrayed, is terrified about what will happen while I am gone.

She confronts me with a tear-splattered wrangle with fangs. Bitterness and jealousy rear their creative heads even after I launch into the pitch about maternity leaves.

The fifteen-year friendship and partnership teeters.

I swing forward into action despite the depth of the pit below. I ask permission to take a leave from the big guy in command on Madison Avenue. I even find a short-term freelance designer replacement to sit in. The boss says I can go if it's okay with my sister-close colleague, who will have to carry the ball while I'm gone. Of course it is not okay with her. I can do her work, but she can't do mine. She's not a designer, she's a copywriter, and I see the writing is already on the wall. In a tone laced with razor blades, she suggests that once I go, I should think about returning on a freelance basis, as an hourly consultant. *After fifteen years.*

But I am determined to do it.

This is a Peace Corps dream, a late-in-lifetime chance: Jewish woman advertising art director/designer goes to Amman to help Palestinian refugee women stand on their own economic feet. A public-relations coup for any agency with brains. Only my agency is bottom-line oriented. They are not thinking it's good business to sponsor Middle East peace agreements, especially if it's on the Arab side of the fence. Besides, most of the agency's clients have medical centers and university dormitories already named for them on every corner of real estate in Israel. They don't know how to handle the change of territory.

My mother is terrified I'll lose the security of my job and its life-supporting income.

"Don't do it," she warns.

The Captain is behind me one hundred percent—as long as I negotiate the terms.

"Do it," he says.

So I do, because if I don't do it, I'll have to keep doing what I have already been doing for fifteen years. And I've done it.

But what I don't do is negotiate the terms.

In the meantime, my colleague is sure I'll never come back and is worried into a nervous state about losing her own job. So while I'm gone, she reconfigures the design group so she becomes the creative director.

And I become history.

FAIR SHARE

But let me back up a few months, long before the job in Jordan is even a twinkle in my eye.

It is autumn in New England.

Although I have the vacation days coming to me, it does seem I haven't been in the office much. We have a commercial to shoot in France at the end of September, two separate client meetings late in October and November in Paris, all of this on top of a quick add-on weekend trip to Tel Aviv for personal reasons. And the Christmas holiday to London and Jordan is just two months away.

Now, understand, when the Captain and I are on the move in the south of France, in Paris, London, Israel, we are not sailing on a boat, although the Captain makes sure to check out every harbor and coastline in the neighborhood. Some people think cell phones ringing nonstop mean you're important. For me, it's the amount of stamps in my passport. For the Captain, it's the amount of ports he can call on. Like a dog and a fire hydrant, he just can't help himself.

So I haven't been in the office a lot, even though I've been working overtime on the road. My sister-close colleague doesn't like this one little bit because she can't get the clients to pay for her to join me on these trips. She's the copy director, not the design director, and although she could capably art-direct the location shoots, she's not as much fun, and the results are not the same. She'd also have to share a room with the film director to keep within the client's budget. And she wouldn't like that. And I wouldn't like that.

The envy is also green because of the inequity of our paychecks.

I think the pearl necklace loses its clasp on a hot September afternoon when she is frantically trying to reach me in St. Paul de Vence at a phone number I give her that isn't working and I don't know it.

The Captain loves the telephone, phone booths, *fone* cards, portable phones. He is annoyed the hotel-room phone is out of order, but it doesn't keep him away from the international operator. He always phones home no matter where he is, and lopes off to the village square to find the one public phone booth, leaving me drenched across the matrimonial-size bed in a room that also doesn't come with air-conditioning. When he calls his studio, he checks in with my office at the same time and gets an earful. He is involved anyway, because he is the hired film director for this location shoot. What is initially supposed to be a long weekend vacation for the two of us, I guiltily agree to turn into a paying job since we're already in the neighborhood.

Sometimes I talk my clients into buying off on more than I can chew.

My sister-close colleague holding down the fort back at the office in the States tells him, *"I want to talk to her now!"* There are client issues with the models for the following week's commercial in France that need fixing, even though it is a Friday afternoon and almost the weekend.

He lopes back to the room. "She sounds upset."

I am jet-lagged. I don't have the energy to even think about walking into town in the breathless heat to call her back.

"I'm not going," I insist. "It's too hot. She'll just have to wait."

The Captain shakes his head. *"I don't know."*

The truth is, I really don't want to deal with anything— with my job, which is meat-grinding me, with my sister-close colleague, whom I feel I am carrying like an extra cosmetic bag on my right arm aching with tendonitis. I don't want to share anymore. She (*we*) wants to share everything: my ideas, my adventures, my style, even my troubles. Whatever is on my plate always looks tastier. Some people at work actually call us "The Sisters" even though we are opposite colors. She is very, very tiny; a porcelain-skinned, plum-black-haired, exotic-looking Asian-American, elegantly black-fashioned, immaculately put together, detail-oriented, outwardly in-control manager type who sharpens all her pencils so the yellow parts are exactly the same length. She is desperate for a Michelin four-star rating for her portion of the menu and pushes her miniature self into every pot I cook up. She is hungry for credit. I know she is hurt and bitter because everyone thinks I am the core ingredient of our design success, and I understand her envy because I usually get all the licks. But she tends to forget I also take all the lickings from the big boss when the engraved award plaques don't cover the bottom line on the profit-and-loss sheet.

It's too bad. We are a team for a very long time. She does the details, I do the big picture. She does the words. I do the concepts. Sometimes it's the other way around. She massages the clients, I pump the heart. She does the hand-holding, I do the hand-tugging. She is serious. I am ridiculous. I am ambitious. She is content. I am driven. She drives a Volvo.

Lately I feel I am being choked to death by a climbing kudzu weed. Or like "Rappaccini's Daughter," a delicate flower with poison petals is inhaling my breath.

I don't really plan it at the time, but the garden is about to be uprooted.

ALL OVER THE PLACE

ISRAEL, ENGLAND, FRANCE, JORDAN

This is already a very complicated year.

My fifteen-year-old daughter is smack in the middle of the nasty teenage years, and all parties agree she might benefit from a school experience far from the bright lights of Boston. She leaves for Israel at the end of the summer to join an American high-school kibbutz program at an Israeli settlement five kilometers from the new Jordanian border crossing. In this environment, she can work with ostriches, camels, and pelicans at the kibbutz zoo when she is not sleeping through class.

In October, the Captain donates a generous amount of frequent-flier miles to my account so I can fly over and check in on her.

I visit for a few days.

There is a *Lord of the Flies* appearance to the student living arrangements on the kibbutz that worries me, but not that much. I am not surprised by what I find because I come of age on a kibbutz myself and think the communal experience is good for the character. I see my daughter is thriving, finding her way, even if her room is the center of the class's small un-washed social universe. Never mind the smells of cigarette butts, sweaty-feet work boots, fermenting plastic bags of sour milk, and the aging cheese scent of dirty socks and underwear whiffing up from under the unmade bed she might be sharing with God knows who.

Kibbutz life is heaven for kids and dogs. I give her a year to get her halo back. The distractions are few and far between, and now she's nowhere near a T stop to take her into Harvard Square to hang with runaway teenagers and skaters in the pit behind the Out of Town News kiosk.

Because my daughter is now in the neighborhood, our very close Jordanian friends across the border in Amman invite all three of us (the Captain, my daughter, and me) to spend Christ-mas vacation with them exploring the archaeological wonders of Petra. Since a December holiday in the Middle East affords another excuse to return and keep my eyes on my daughter's education, and because the Captain and I are going to be in London for his Hastings School rugby reunion anyway, we agree after that to fly a little farther east. At the time, I don't think it is at all strange that we are two Jewish girls and one lapsed Catholic man celebrating Greek Orthodox Christmas at a Nabatean ruin in a Muslim country with a wealthy Palestinian-exiled family.

But it is not this simple.

The Captain's impossible-to-please, ailing father decides to start dying two days into the London leg of our Christmas trip a year after the Duchess surprises everyone by dying first. This is typical of the demanding old man.

"You need to fly down and be with him," I advise. "He must be terrified to be dying all alone."

"But the reunion dinner!" The Captain despairs. "I've waited thirty years to see these guys."

Blood, however, is thicker than love.

I want to stay by the Captain's side, but I am not invited along to lend support because his father doesn't like me, especially when he's dying.

The Captain leaves me to continue on alone to Israel and flies to France to be with his father for the bitter end. He is just in time. As the Ambassador lies dazed and confused, moved home to his penthouse bedroom to keep him from dying in his hospital bed at the last minute, he is still sharp enough to tell his only son he shouldn't show up without an appointment.

The clock is ticking.

The old man is determined to upstage the old boys in London and lingers on through the late afternoon.

"If I leave now, I can make it," debates the Captain, checking his watch while calculating the gain of an extra hour of Greenwich Mean Time.

He doesn't waste a minute.

The Captain races back to London just in time to put the napkin in his lap for the first course of his reunion dinner. He plans to jet right back to his father's bedside, after the last testimonial, but now he is running later than the planes. The continental call from his father's valet comes in the middle of cigars and nightcaps. In a stuttering mix of French and market-stall English, the valet tearfully breaks the news. He says the Honorable Ambassador dies peacefully in his sleep after the private nurse assures him no one is stealing the silver.

The Captain catches the first flight back to France in the morning. He finds the private nurse laying fresh linens on the now empty bed, having swept away all the hospital trimmings down the service elevator along with the retired Ambassador.

"Thank God I missed that," the Captain calls, direct-dialing me in northern Galilee, "but I worked out a great opening line for the eulogy I'd like to run by you. It's from Mark Twain. It starts something like this. *'When I was a boy of fourteen, my father was so ignorant I could hardly stand to have the old man around. But when I got to be twenty-one, I was astonished at how much the old man had learned in seven years.'* "

There is a pause.

"It's good, isn't it?"

"I think you need your sons," I advise from the public telephone at the kibbutz dining hall. "I'd like to be with you, too. It's not a problem. I'll catch the next flight."

"You're absolutely right about the boys," he agrees quickly. "But I think I am fine here on my own without you . . . it's complicated, you know. Look, I'll catch up to you in Jordan on Christmas. You're okay with this, right?"

What can I say?

In a flurry of credit-card activity, he flies his five sons from both coasts of the States over to the south of France for their grandfather's memorial service. The stage is neatly set for the closing act.

He calls me again two minutes before the chapel doors close.

"It's just immediate family and very close friends, you understand," he updates from the corridor. "By the way, can you believe I contacted my father's embassy and they didn't even send a representative?"

"It's not the same government," I remind him.

The organ pipes up a dirge in the background.

"Gotta run," he signs off. "I'll call you later."

That same afternoon, the five sons and their father sprinkle the Honorable Ambassador's ashes somewhere up near *La Haute Corniche* where Princess Grace runs off the road, leaving her fairy-tale principality behind without a happy ending. After a late lunch, they return to the Belle Époque apartment to sift through a century of debris.

"Don't leave without changing the locks," is the smart piece of long-distance advice my mother doles out with her three-minute sympathy call.

The Captain listens to her. It's only a precaution to keep the wolves away from the second-tier Dutch Master oils hanging on the Oriental yellow silk-covered drawing-room walls until they are faithfully distributed to their rightful heirs.

He calls in the royal locksmiths.

An hour before his flight to catch up with me in the Middle East, he hands the newly minted keys over to the private bank executor of his late father's late second wife's carefully inventoried estate. The loyal servants stand lined up at attention by the front door.

The cook's eyes grow moist. *"But I must be allowed in to walk ze dog!"*

The cook gets a hefty allowance. And the dog.

"Monsieur le Capitaine," lisps the loyal valet with tearing

eyes, "I shall miss the old monsieur. *Who will polish the Ambassador's silver?*"

The Captain offers the valet a silver spoon—an oversized ivory-crested envelope stuffed with thousand-franc notes garnished with an ounce of gold from the Ambassador's prized cuff link collection.

"Oh, monsieur," weeps the valet.

Taking only what is left to him, the Captain stuffs his own deceased mother's diamond tiara and his father's Patek Philippe platinum-gold wristwatch into his shaving kit, shuts the heavy door firmly behind him, and hits the road.

Dusty and crumpled after a five-hour-long land border crossing from Israel into Jordan, I reach Amman a few hours before the Captain's scheduled arrival. I sign both the Captain's and my names in at the hotel reception, then follow an underage Bedouin bellboy up three flights to inspect the room. The room is clean. There is even water coming out of the shower tap.

"It's fine," I approve.

"You are welcome." The bellboy backs out of the door, leaving behind an unwashed scent.

I shower. I nap, I hang around, I wait. In two hours a hired driver is scheduled to pick the Captain up at the international airport an hour south of the city and drive him to the capital. I count on an additional forty-five minutes with rush-hour traffic.

Checking my watch, I calculate I have just enough time to rush to downtown Amman for some last-minute textile shopping before the *souk* closes and get back to the hotel before the Captain's anticipated time of arrival.

I hail a taxi outside the hotel.

"First Circle, please," I direct.

It is late Thursday afternoon. In the heart of the crumbling remains of the old city, a crush of donkey carts, veiled women, white-robed men, and untended children clog the market streets. I elbow my way through jammed alleyways teeming with hopeful shopkeepers insisting I stop and consider their sacks of dried spices, hanging slabs of sheep, shining brassware, or to simply slow down and smell their fresh-ground coffee. Keeping tab of the time, I ignore the seductive welcomes and nose forward into the shadowy depths of the silk market.

By the second shop on the fourth alleyway, I get caught up in bargaining negotiations over the price of five meters of *Siyah,* a damascene-striped silk weave not found anywhere else on earth except next door in off-limits Syria. The proud proprietor waters down my resistance with glass after glass of mint-leaf tea.

This piece of business could take all day.

The muezzin at the city mosque calls in the arriving sunset with a wail of the loudspeaker. Prayer rugs are unrolled. The faithful kneel.

I look at my watch. The hour has slipped by.

"Okay, I'll take it," I agree. "*Shukran.*"

The silk merchant raises his robed arm and curls his finger and thumb together in a holding signal. He nods at me most politely, whisks out a one-man, well-worn Persian carpet from behind the battered wooden counter, and unfurls the mat onto the earthen floor. Turning his back to the west, he sinks to his knees.

In Jordan, time does not fly on Persian carpets.

Evening prayers could take all night.

And politeness counts.

I wait.

The return trip to the hotel at the other end of the city takes more time than I have.

A tipped-over coffee vendor's cart floods the bottom of the *Jebel Amman* outbound road with a sludge of muddy grinds, holding up all traffic and my taxi until each rolling thimble-size ceramic coffee cup is restored to the teetering stack being collected by the arm-flailing proprietor.

It is Christmas Eve as well as the beginning of the Muslim weekend.

Anxious city drivers drape over their steering wheels, hitting their polished horns like heralds. Everyone who is everyone is driving a diesel-fueled Mercedes. The traffic jam is impressive. Muslim, Christian, Jewish—we all share a common goal, to get out of town before sundown. And we are all in a hurry.

I coach my taxi driver through the First and Second Circles, holding a pocketful of coins in my hand for encouragement. Only when he careens left at the intersection to an outlying suburb a few traffic lights away from the hotel do I dare check my watch.

I have eighteen minutes left of spare change.

When we screech to a halt by the hotel entrance, I clutch the heavy brown paper package of cloth to my chest and fumble with a well-worn wad of Jordanian dinars.

"May Allah bless you." I thank the driver and pay him handsomely.

"*Tdfadal.*" He nods heroically.

A hotel doorman opens the taxi door for my exit and bows as if I am the arriving wife of a senior diplomat.

"*Madame,*" the hotel concierge says, winking, as I rush to the front desk to ask for the room key. "*Your husband is already upstairs.*"

The Captain is not pleased when I announce myself at the door.

"*Is it too much to expect you to be here for me!?*" he demands with an ambassadorial tone when I rush into the suite to greet him with open arms five minutes too late.

DIVINE RETRIBUTION

FIRST CIRCLE, AMMAN

Spring forward to March.

The fax is on the chair in my office. My fate is written. I am off to Jordan for more than a holiday.

I rent a spacious apartment in First Circle, Amman, opposite the pasha-style Saudi Arabian embassy, in the oldest and most atmospheric district of the city. My bedroom windows look directly onto the submachine guns of the Jordanian soldiers protecting the white-robed diplomats who whirl in and out of the embassy at all hours of the day and night.

The owners of the apartment are only too glad to have me inhabit their original family homestead and look after the dust-covered stretch of well-furnished rooms they leave behind when they move to a better neighborhood. They are very impressed to have someone working under the patronage of the queen living under their old roof, and even supply me with a Filipino maid to keep the place free of desert dust. They don't care that I'm Jewish. They only care that I can pay the rent.

Once the epicenter of the wealthy elite near the bottom of the main hill of the seven that make up the ancient city of Philadelphia, First Circle is no longer considered the place to live. I can't understand why. I can walk the five blocks to my work at the foundation showroom. The buildings in my neighborhood have great character, if somewhat crumbling, and remind me of vintage Jerusalem with the Islamic core untouched. The old British Cultural Center, Hashem's dirty but delicious falafel-and-hummus trattoria, the books@café, the Royal Hashemite Palace and Court, and a lot of available taxis are just a mortar's throw from the Roman Amphitheater and the crowded, colorful markets that make the downtown down.

I think it's a perfect location.

I am not alone in this opinion.

Along with the meager water that trickles out of the faucets of my 1930s-style bathroom's deep white procelain bathtub, matching sink, and bidet, I am startled from a half sleep during my middle-of-the-night bathroom trips by scurrying underfoot. In the middle of feeling my way over the white tile wall to the toilet-paper holder, I snap on the light. The floor moves with activity. I gasp midflush. Dozens of cockroaches are scurrying up over the sides of the tub, crawling into the sink basin, running down the waterspout, up the toilet tank— all moving even faster than their evolution into the twentieth century.

And they are not plastic.

When the Captain flies over to Amman to visit me during spring vacation week, I warn him about the company in the bathroom at night. This interests him.

"They're real," I whisper in his ear our first night snuggled together in bed, and beg him to scout out the bathroom before I go in. I've already sprinkled a heavy dose of poison powder all along the tiles, but the body count still shocks me.

"Please check first," I beg him. "Just this once."

He thinks for a minute.

Rolling onto his back, he puts his hands behind his head. There is a stretched-out silence. I lean up on one elbow and give him a questioning look.

"No," he answers when the long pause breaks into a deliberate statement.

"You're kidding?"

"No. I'm not."

I don't really blame him. I know exactly what he is thinking when he stays firmly under the covers and outwaits me to absolutely have to visit the bathroom before he does. I know what he is thinking when he finally hears me gasp to find the cockroaches lying half dead on their backs, legs squirming in the air in battle fatigue.

He is thinking with biblical satisfaction, *Divine Retribution.*

THE END (AGAIN)

TRICK QUESTION

Sometime at the beginning of our relationship, long before the Captain becomes a captain, I once ask him this question:

Q: *"If you could invite anyone for dinner, alive or dead, whom would you choose?"*

I have already thought through my own list:

1. Solo Guest: *Adolf Hitler*
2. Table for Six: *Adolf Hitler, Moshe Dayan, Golda Meir, Ben Gurion, Yonah Steiner, and me.*

The Captain considers the question for a few seconds.

"Anyone?" he asks. "Historical or fiction?"

I nod.

His answer takes only a second more.

"You," he says.

I am taken by surprise. I feel warm and mushy inside, and guilty for not having thought to put him on my list.

I don't believe him, but I really do.

It is a decade later.

We are seated side by side at the Captain's table in the ship's galley, sky dark, wind howling topsides, we are so close our plates are touching. Empty wineglasses ring the red-ribbed place mats, and the moment is romantic.

It is New Year's Eve. I don't know it yet, but it is our last holiday together.

I ask him:

Q: *"If you could invite anyone for dinner, alive or dead, whom would you ask?"*

He stops and considers the question as if hearing it for the first time. "Anyone?" he asks. "Historical or fiction?"

I nod.

He thinks. He deliberates. He mulls over a list I can't see.

When he answers, I can't really remember what he says.

Maybe he names Edith Piaf or Winston Churchill.

All I can remember is the answer isn't *"you."*

I tell him I'm hurt that I don't make the list.

"But you're already here," he says quickly, dismissing my feelings with a swat at a mosquito.

I believe him, but I really don't.

THE FRENCH KISS

(Chapters to write, but I don't feel like it:)
Police-Station-French-Lessons
The Missing Blue Blazer
One Last Christmas
Sailing on Thin Ice
Charleston Chills
Savannah Sweats
Blazerless in Beaufort
New Year's Cake Overboard

THE LAST TRIP

We've been apart yet again for another three months.

"You work while I sail" is the unspoken agreement. The Captain has been cruising down along the southern coast to Florida throughout the winter. I've been working in Boston trying to launch my new studio. Although the Captain is just about to turn back up the coast toward home, Best Buddy reminds him of a ten-day sailing cruise commitment on the Chesapeake he preregistered them for a year ago.

"Sail with me on the cruise," the Captain invites long distance. "Fly down to the boat. I'll buy the ticket."

"I don't know . . ." I hesitate.

It's a difficult time to get away. I have a teenage daughter finishing her junior year in high school, a toddling business on the verge of walking, a handful of anxious clients, and a voice-of-doom mother with a very long phone cord.

"I'd really like you to come," the Captain adds as the connection starts to break up. "It's only for ten days. Please. I miss you."

"Okay." I agree reluctantly because I miss him, too. But I don't have a good feeling about it.

I hang up.

The phone rings again. My biggest client is on the line.

"We need you right away," they insist, "to produce ten commercial spots featuring the chairman of the board. They have to be broadcast in two weeks."

The budget is big. Supportive.

I need the Captain.

I reach him six hours later on his mobile phone. I can hear the chug of the diesel engine and the burp of the watery depth sounder on the other end. I quickly explain the project to him.

"Please come up and shoot this job for me? The client wants only the best." I hear myself plead. "After the shoot, we can fly back down to the boat just in time for the cruise."

There is a watery pause.

"Hello? Can you hear me?"

"*I don't feel like it*," he says finally, his voice crackling up in static. "I don't want to leave the boat and fly up."

"It's really important to me," I tell him with rising anger. "I need this job."

"Well, next weekend is Best Buddy's pig roast, the week after is the Memorial Day yacht-club regatta, and then the ten-day offshore cruise. How about waiting until the end of June? I'll give you a day."

"That's six weeks from now!"

"That's my final offer."

"Forget it. I'll just hire another director."

I throw out a few top names and slam the phone down.

He calls right back.

He flies up the next week.

The job gets done.

Only the price is much higher than I expect.

OUT ON
THE CHESAPEAKE

LAST NAMES

CROSSING THE POTOMAC

The sea is sympathetic.

We are cruising across the mouth of a rolling Chesape^
under a cloudless blue sky. We are to meet up with Best F
and the cruising club at a port destination a five-hour ɕ

It is just the two of us on board.

The Captain is stationed below in the gallɕ
other cup of coffee while tuned into the radio sɕ
for Best Buddy's signal.

I am at the helm letting the autopilot do ʄ

There is an awkward unspoken sentence ʂ

Maybe it's just the past three months aɟ
together for Best Buddy's club cruise that
entry distance. Or maybe I'm just imagini

Something is wrong and I am about to make what's wrong not right.

"Can we talk for a few minutes?" I ask carefully.

"What's up?" He lends me half an ear.

"I don't feel comfortable in my name anymore."

I am sure if I could see them, the small gray hairs on the back of his neck would be standing straight up.

"What's wrong with your name?"

"It's the last name that doesn't fit anymore."

"Just use your first."

"That's not a solution."

He is edgy.

I take a deep breath and let it out.

"I don't want to be an aging girlfriend."

"Moon Tiger, Moon Tiger, this is the Jolly Roger, come in." Best Buddy's call cuts through the waves of static.

The Captain leaps to attention, moving the radio microphone to his lips.

"Jolly Roger, Jolly Roger, this is Moon Tiger, over."

"Moon Tiger, Moon Tiger, read me your position."

I can see the Captain's present position even without the GPS headings flashing on the overhead monitor.

And it's different from mine.

SITTING DUCK

POINT LOOKOUT

Can a sneeze trigger a final blowout?

If so, the first tickle of real trouble begins in a harbor-side steamy Chinese restaurant where Best Buddy organizes a group dinner jump-starting the party two nights before the real cruise begins. The invitees show up at port by car and include Best Buddy's stream-of-unconscious family, the only yachting crew he can rope into service and who will also say yes to his social invitations, which also means the Captain, which also means me.

"Dinner onshore at twenty hundred hours," Best Buddy directs. "The best Peking duck in town! I know the owner personally." He wags his finger in my direction, *"Be ready."*

The Captain and Best Buddy make the dry run to the

restaurant from the boat with the first entourage because the car can only fit five. Best Buddy's wife and I are left behind to tidy up our sister boats and powder our armpits in peace until her grown daughter's return with the car to collect us in the second relay.

When we women finally arrive at the restaurant, we are directed to the backdoor entrance.

I admit Best Buddy and the Captain do consider my changing-tables-at-restaurants behavior serious enough to require organizing a banquet-size space in the back of the back room, where smoking is prohibited. It's a corner, at least. But the grinding air conditioner in the front barely lowers the relentless ninety-degree muggy temperature and I feel enormously hot. Even hotter than usual, which lately is not so unusual. My body temperature is swampy, and I am heat-flushed, irritably sensitive to the slightest degree change. I cannot even stand myself, any more the dictates of Best Buddy puffing up about the exquisite direct-from-Peking duck he is ordering to show off his culinary sophistication.

"SIT DOWN, WOMAN!" Best Buddy orders from the corner, waving a half-glass of Scotch and soda.

The Captain motions for me to sit next to him, but the chair faces the wall with its back to the restaurant, an uncomfortable position to be in. I think because he is already deep into his second rum, the Captain won't mind if I move to the chair directly across from him, back to the wall, on the outer edge of the already-in-progress party. He doesn't seem to mind.

So I sit down next to Best Buddy's brother-in-law, whose graphic scars from drastic, multiple skin-cancer operations pulse purple through a radiated, hairless head. That the brother-in-law is sailing without so much as a hat, suntan lotion, or complaint amazes me. I don't think the brother-in-law feels a thing. His hand is wrapped around an empty bourbon glass and he is just ordering another round.

Best Buddy's unflappable wife slips without fuss into the chair by the Captain's side, back facing the room. She positions herself next to her thirty-something daughter, who drops back down beside her thrice-married, thrice-divorced fiancé, a free-lance government operative with security clearance who is just about the same retirement age as Best Buddy. The difference between the fiancé and Best Buddy is that the future-son-in-law speaks in double negatives. Since the entire family is born with upper lips already stiff, British-educated Best Buddy tries to keep his appalled opinions to himself, but I can see the class of this new addition to the family bothers the hell out of him.

The men draw their drinks closer to their bellies and shift their sprawled legs to accommodate the female parts. The appetizers are good, even if they are ordered with great fanfare and horn tooting by Best Buddy. The wheeling-dealing Thai owner/waitress of this authentic Chinese restaurant jollies him along. I am thinking she must have hostess experience with rowdy GIs in Bangkok bars. Or maybe she is hoping for a good tip. Anyway, she probably doesn't realize she's got the wrong man. The Captain usually sponsors these restaurant bills. For the price of dinner, he can afford to sit back, relax, and stir the melting ice in his rum and tonic while Best Buddy takes charge of the menu and any disorderly dissenters.

I should apprentice with Best Buddy's wise and remarkably liberal wife. She looks like the strong, silent type until a one-line zinger makes everyone sit up and take notice. I like her. I admire her. She is an old Smith girl, also from a Social Register family. She grows up "coming about" with the sailing set and takes the whole watery world with the long easy stride of her still great-looking legs. She has been in the club almost as long as Best Buddy, so we're talking all the way back to English boarding-school days. She still keeps up with the Captain's first wife, with whom I'm sure she shares the secrets of the first eighteen years of both their marriages. But that is undoubtedly the extent of her involvement, and she would never tell you, anyway. She is loyal and honor-bound in her commitments, and I know the Captain always comes second, right after Best Buddy, in her allegiance. Even if at times she thinks either of them acts like a horse's ass, she glides through each episode with her monogrammed, timeworn, white blouse unruffled as the day it is handed down to her.

We are settled at the table. I drink my usual, a gin and grapefruit juice with a strong kick, which flushes the heat higher. After a few sips, I feel funny, as if perhaps my head will blow up off the table and squirt blood on the pink tablecloth. I ignore the body heat and sample a pancake concoction of Peking duck and scallions, then launch into hot spicy filet mignon cubes coated with peanuts doused with caramelized chili peppers.

"Did I tell you that Sir Edward wants us to crew for him on next year's race to Ireland? Five weeks across the Atlantic." Best Buddy catty-corners the Captain with this announcement. "Are you in?"

I sneeze.

I don't catch the Captain's answer.

"Well, let's make sure to provision the boat with real food this time." Best Buddy starts planning. "None of that Spam swill."

I sneeze again.

At this moment I am listening to Best Buddy lecture on the bad manners of a particular aristocratic French sailor with a glamorous yacht who has the nerve to treat Best Buddy like a common galley boy during an offshore cruise to Bermuda.

The third sneeze removes me entirely from the conversation.

I feel like Alice falling through a wind tunnel and watch as the distance between the Captain and me grows longer than the width of the table. He is so involved with Best Buddy's rehashing of the French put-down, he doesn't notice my distress.

Suddenly, from my deepening tunnel, a bell rings in my head. Startling me like a too late wake-up call, I wonder what the hell I am doing here with these people.

And then I stop breathing.

The lack of oxygen takes me by force, squeezing my lungs into a tight fist, and I look across the table, horrified I am going to die right then and there and can't even tell the Captain because he will think I need attention. My lungs can't lasso in the air. They are stuck. My ears burn hot, my scalp rushes red with blood, and my skin crawls as if I am swimming in, and now smothered by, itchy pink fiberglass insulation. I hear my little inner voice piping up through the panic telling me *this is it*, in one more second I am going to keel over and turn blue. And I know that whether I can breathe or not is less important than if the Captain will be embarrassed if I cause a health scene right there at the table.

It is a terrifying sensation, to stop breathing. I don't think anyone at the table is aware of what is not going on in my lungs. Desperately, I look over to the Captain for help, my eyes wide with alarm. But he has this I-need-to-please-the-crowd face on and isn't available.

This is not a man who will be there for me when I die, is all I can think. He will believe I am making it up. I tell myself not to be a hypochondriac. That it is not serious. That I can breathe. That I should just stop eating these nuts, this hot dish. That I should slow down; it will pass. I tell myself to pretend I am just swimming and am holding my breath underwater. It will pass.

I'm right; it passes.

My lungs release and fill with air. The relief overwhelms me with gratitude for not having to make a scene.

But the panic remains. Only Best Buddy catches on. His eyebrows lift above the rim of his glasses, his eyes knowingly graze mine.

"I'll outlast you!" Best Buddy announces to me from the head of the table in a grand finale toast.

On board that night, I dream a horrible dream that I am tangled underwater in churning seaweed and am drowning. In the dream, the Captain swims away. I can't remember all the details now, but I want to wake the Captain up and tell him about it, to tell him how I almost die at dinner. But he is thick with sleep and I think twice about disturbing him. I shiver awake from the dream with a to-the-bone chill. I am suddenly freezing, which at first feels delicious, then becomes absolutely unbearable. I lie frozen for a while and consider all the alternatives. I cannot get warm under my own covers. He is wrapped up in his quilt, an arm out of reach. But extra guest quilts are stowed up forward in the hold. I decide to get one. I tug a quilt out of its tight position from under the iron-link anchor chain and struggle to pull it out from its protective plastic bag cover.

When I finally succeed, I throw the blanket over both of us, warm myself up from the effort, and eventually fall asleep.

In the morning, the Captain is distant and moody. If he has a hangover, he won't tell me, but gets critical, instead, for not waking him up in the night to ask permission before I make a mess of the guest quilts looking for warmth.

I don't know it at the time, but this is our last day together.

THE LAUNDRY BAG

THE MARINA

The temperature continues to rise.

I am dragging and lagging. He is pacing and racing.

I think it is a good idea to do laundry at the marina before our club cruise boat leaves port because I find myself left with one pair of salty shorts and two soggy T-shirts and nothing to wear for the evening's gala kickoff barbecue. Which is why, I realize, my sail bag is so light when I reach to grab it from the airport carousel. I think I have packed lightly and hope the Captain notices, but this morning, as things start heating up, I discover I've forgotten to pack the bottom half of my clothes. I see them still lying in a pile on my bed in Boston.

I grab a handful of change, collect the dirty towels, my few used clothes, wrap myself in an old sarong, and head off down the dock. As I pass by Best Buddy's sister boat, I am even offered one of his third-day worn white polo shirts to throw into the wash cycle. When I bump into the Captain en route from a garbage run and ask if he needs anything washed, he is annoyed and grumpy.

"I don't need to do laundry."

"I'll take care of it," I tell him.

And I do. I carry the laundry and powder and use my own quarters. I sit in the stuffy two-machine utility room watching the cycles so I don't lose my turn. The Captain drifts off outside under a tree with the Sunday paper.

I am standing directly in front of the machine, switching loads, wiping the perspiration from my upper lip, when a midlife, Bermuda-shorted, pink-polo-shirted sailing wife wearing pink espadrilles with matching painted pink toenails strides in. I have never seen her before. She brushes past me carrying a wicker basket, snatches my load from the tumbler, and tosses my wet laundry onto the back of a dirty white plastic chair, then fills the tub with her wet laundry.

"Excuse me," I say, my voice rumpled with indignation, "I am using this machine."

"Well, you're using one machine too many." Her accent is British, her manner entitled. "I absolutely must dry my clothes *now.*"

Imperious and intimidating, she looks me up and down, sizing up my faded sarong and bare feet. I can see her ranking my class, dismissing me as if I am off a triple-decker powerboat. I am too hot to match her entitlement and am surprised at my lack of forceful response. Instead, I back silently out of the steamy utility room and cross the lawn to tell the Captain about the laundry delay, but he catches me first and waves me over to his chair, where he is still reading the Sunday paper.

"Come meet this great couple," he says, tossing the paper I haven't had a chance to look at yet into the trash barrel. "They'll be sailing with us on the cruise. They're British. You'll like her, she's wonderful," he says. "She's sailed all the way across the Atlantic with her husband."

He leads me back toward the clubhouse veranda. But I am looking beyond the deck, up the stairs to the laundry room.

"See that aging blond woman over there," I whisper. "The one wearing the dreadful hot-pink espadrilles who's just walking out of the laundry room, the one with that short man with the blue fake yachting cap?"

"Yes, that's the couple I want you to meet." He sounds confused.

"They're on this cruise?" I am appalled.

I don't have a chance to tell the Captain about her bad manners in the laundry room because the short man with the blue fake yachting cap suddenly steps forward to greet the Captain, smiling broadly like a lifelong friend. The pink-espadrilled wife beams a hello, then gives the Captain a startled look when he introduces me. The British wife's hot-pink lipstick is melting now into an uncomfortable smile.

"This is the woman in my life," the Captain introduces me to the surprised couple.

Clearly I am not off a powerboat.

"We've met," I say dryly, retying the knot on my sagging sarong.

"Oh, I didn't know . . ." she stutters at first, then regains her composure ". . . *you were with us.*"

But I am not going to be for much longer.

THE LAST KISS

TIED UP

It's the same day, only now it is late afternoon.

We have argued about hiking into town to buy extra bourbon for Best Buddy's brother-in-law. We have quarreled over making icebox room to keep my seven-grains bread from getting yeasty. It is either bread or tonic water. To the Captain, there is no choice.

We are now tucked below in the heart of the forepeak. After a long hot afternoon under the southern Chesapeake sun, enduring Best Buddy's whipping cattle drive to make the twin boats shipshape for this evening's gala barbecue event and tomorrow's cruise, I coax the Captain into a late-afternoon nap. He is grateful for permission to rest.

"You take care of the boat, and I'll take care of you," I tell him. But I can see I'm the one who is breaking down.

Before his exhausted eyes flutter shut, he looks at me with a boyish bashfulness. *"I love you."* He says my name with an intimate tone deep from his chest under the hand that rests above his heart.

I am surprised.

I lean over to kiss him on his sunburned forehead. He reaches up to pull me closer.

"Ahoy! Permission to come aboard?" interrupts Best Buddy, stomping topsides onto the deck.

I send the Captain one desperate look of discouragement.

The Captain lets go of my hand and edges out of the tight bunk, wiping the fatigue from his face.

"Permission granted," he calls up the companionway.

"Cocktails onboard at eighteen-hundred hours!" Best Buddy bellows. "You guys provide the boat. We'll bring the party."

"What is the time now?" asks the Captain, dragging a perk to his voice.

Best Buddy checks his watch. "Seventeen-thirty hours. You have exactly thirty minutes."

"We'll be ready."

THE LAST SUPPER

DOCKSIDE

18:00 Hours

I'm not ready.

I need a shower.

"Can I dash into the head for a quick rinse?" I request. "Please?"

The Captain is irritated. The ship's bell is just chiming cocktail hour. My onboard shower will soap up the head. Cruise guests are due on board for a tour and a drink at any minute. My belated rinse is not good nautical etiquette.

"I wish you wouldn't," he grumbles, "but you're going to do what you need to do, anyway."

And I do.

Cocktails: 18:02

We have visitors. I hear well-mannered *ahoys,* and *welcome on board* noises on the other side of the head door. I try to make it snappy. After a quick rinse, I squeeze around the door and extend a dripping hand to a husband-and-wife team.

"Hi," I say, "nice to meet you," even though it isn't.

He is gray and attractive in a Morgan Stanley way. She is dull and dumpy in a trailing-behind way.

The Captain makes the introductions with a bright smile. "This is not just any sailor," he prefaces. "He's done the Arctic Route." The Captain's admiration is as true-blue as our guest's polo shirt.

"Weren't you cold?" I ask incredulously.

"Well, yes," answers the Arctic Sailor with surprise. "As a matter of fact, we had to cut right through ice blocks and glaciers. Absolutely frigid."

Our guest is just warming up with survival stories.

"And you?" I ask the wife. "Did you sail the Arctic with him?"

"Me? Oh no. I couldn't. I had to stay home and look after our grandchildren."

Appetizers: 19:00

On the lawn outside the marina clubhouse, a half-dozen picnic tables covered in red checkerboard plastic tablecloths are set with hungry man-size compartmentalized plastic plates. Red-plastic Dixie drinking cups filled with a white plastic fork, knife, and spoon wrapped inside a paper napkin decorate each setting.

The long planked picnic tables, lined up in banquet formation, remind me uncomfortably of da Vinci's *Last Supper* seating arrangement.

The air is still and steamy.

Southern mosquitoes wait politely under the boathouse wings for the setting sun to announce their invitation to dine. The feast—forty-eight succulent midlife sailors in short-sleeve, blue polo shirts and khaki-colored Bermuda shorts, along with a matching set of red-bliss-potato-skinned retired boat wives boiled a little too long in the sun—is about to begin. Dinner is prepaid by the cruising-club members and comes complete with smoked barbecue chicken breasts, charred-to-perfection pulled pork ribs, a salad tossed with iceberg lettuce, a suspect over-mayonnaised coleslaw, and a human sacrifice for dessert.

The Captain is in his element swapping sailing stories and holding court. His left hand clutches a lukewarm bottle of beer while his right hand pumps greetings with new members as if he is a vote-collecting politician. Best Buddy and his wife are marking their own social territory two picnic tables away.

The Captain, when I tug his arm to remind him I am there, introduces me to a handful of beaming club members.

"Meet the woman in my life." He puts his big hand on my shoulder and nudges me forward into the circle of duplicate-bearded boat skippers and fading-rose wives. The Captain diplomatically searches for a connecting thread. "I'm sure you women have a lot in common."

I'm sure we don't.

I look face-to-wrinkled-face at the aging boat wives.

This is my future, I think. And I do not like it.

And I do not like them.

I release the Captain's hand from mine and evaporate into the humidity.

Across the lawn, I notice the British Couple buttonholing an unattended pair of senior sailors. By this hour, I have carefully circulated the story of the dryer-snatching wife to anyone within earshot. I am gratified with the result; anyone who is anyone is horrified. The seed is planted and there is more than enough fertilizer.

"I know exactly what you mean," inserts one insulted senior cruise member's bristling wife. "We tried to show our American Southern hospitality and invited them for a home-cooked meal last week. And do you know, she never, ever, once said thank you, or even admired my garden?"

The British Couple are dumped like harbor tea.

Palate Cleanser: 19:30

While the party moves from the lawn to the picnic tables, I take a break to run up to the clubhouse to phone home. My sweet-sixteen daughter should be on the other end of the line, or at least the baby-sitter. There is no answer. Not even a dog bark.

Worried, I call my mother instead.

This is a mistake.

"You should be home with your daughter," she lectures. "Maybe the Captain can afford to run around the Chesapeake, but *you* have a child to support and a business to run!"

She pushes all the wrong buttons because she is absolutely right.

There are five more cruise days out to sea. Then another

eight-hour day sail back to our southern starting port, all to catch a local county prop plane back to the big city airport I am certain is just a bird's-eye view from where we are presently docked.

Suddenly I am terrified. I cannot get home from here. I cannot get home from there. I cannot even get home from where we shall be sailing to because the Captain is not planning on shore leave. The only plan he has worked out is to leave me on someone else's boat while he continues his additional three-week offshore haul back to the cold waters of New England and home.

I feel as if the life-raft line to safety has been cut.

Entrées: 19:45

The Captain has drifted away. I find him settled with his dinner plate at a front-row picnic table chatting up a blue-haired lady from Arkansas who looks delighted with his company. I feel hurt that he goes on to dine without looking for me. My independent spirit collapses. I find myself wandering around and around the circle of food-laden buffet trays, empty plastic plate in hand, feeling as if the compass of my life has suddenly been demagnetized.

I try to catch his eye.

But he is not looking my way.

The Captain has just launched into a sailing story I have heard too many times. He is smiling and performing with expert timing. His audience is mesmerized. He is sailing them through fierce tidal waves of hurricane seas with a mast snapped in half by a bolt of lightning. Against all odds, he edges them away from the near-death coordinates of the Bermuda Triangle and navigates to safety with only a broken rudder and the grace of God. At this highlight, the Captain catches his breath, pauses as the listeners exhale a collective sigh of down-to-the-wire relief, then he rescues the entire table by refreshing everyone's drinks.

In the background twilight, I am single-handedly helping myself to a breast of Southern barbecued chicken and a scoop of potato salad. Balancing the chicken breast on the dividing ridges of the plastic dinner plate, I try to swallow the rising panic. Searching for safety, I gratefully squeeze in next to the sympathetic wife of another sailing buddy, who generously makes room for me on the bench at the Captain's table. She greets me with a warm smile and a big hug and confesses that she, too, is feeling left out. *"At least we have each other,"* she whispers.

The table fills up with regulars and new members, and the buzz of conversation lulls me into complacency.

"The Captain's girlfriend is Jewish," says someone from the far end of the picnic table.

"What's that?" I perk up at the sound of my name.

I look up from my plate and am confused for a moment until I realize the sympathetic wife's sensitive sailing-buddy husband at the far end of the table is trying to brush over the subject, because I am the subject.

There is an uncomfortable hush around the table.

"She wants to tell a Jewish joke," the sensitive husband clues me in, pointing to the blue-haired Arkansas lady with a distinctly born-again Christian drawl chatting up the Captain on the other side of the table. "I just thought she should know you are Jewish. That's all."

"What's this?" I ask, confused by the sudden shift in table conversation.

"It's just the funniest Jewish joke." The Arkansas woman persists, looking for the group's blessing.

I lean across the table and direct my voice to the hosting Captain, who seems genuinely puzzled by the knot in the conversation.

"Let's pass on this joke," I suggest. "I think only Jews should tell jokes about Jews."

"But it isn't offensive at all!!" insists the Arkansas lady, showing a yellowing set of bridgework.

I am already offended.

"Please, don't do this." I submit my formal request to the Captain.

He looks at me blankly, then turns his head to nod permission, dismissing my distress with a pleasing smile to the woman-stranger.

"Go on," he prompts, "it's okay. Tell it to me. I'll tell her the joke later."

There is no turning back.

She leaps forward with the joke, stunning even the other twelve diners seated around the picnic table with her determination.

Q: *"Do you know what a Jewish dilemma is?"*

There is a short pause.

A: *"Free ham!"* She chortles.

I am horrified.

I burn.

I almost don't listen to the joke. But I do. And now I'm trying to ignore the punch line, the guffaws, the half chuckles. Until my ears prick up to hear the Captain, my own side, the love of my life, poking the same blue-haired lady on the shoulder, adding without a skip in the beat, "Did you hear the joke about the three Jewish mothers from Miami?"

The Captain completely ignores my shocked face.

"No. Don't." I throw him a last-chance plea from my side of the splintered table.

"It's okay," the Captain pronounces as he tells the table, "her father told me the joke the other night."

And while I am trying desperately hard not to listen, he plunges on.

I do everything not to listen, except to the laughs at the end.

The joke's a hit.

But with the wrong audience.

In his performance to make the group of sailing strangers comfortable, to smooth over their discomfort at my discomfort, the Captain jettisons thirteen years of our intimate relationship straight into the Chesapeake Bay with a punch that has taken me to the end of the line.

"I don't believe he did that," consoles my sympathetic wife friend.

I am unable to digest the facts right there.

"I've got to go," I tell her.

I cannot look at the Captain as I push off from the table. I can only hear him laughing and pleasing the crowd.

The sun is just setting, but I can feel my face beat purple with the heat of humiliation. I disappear from the picnic-table social and slink down the docks toward the boat.

Back on board, I pace the cockpit while the sympathetic wife gently offers support. I steam. I agonize. I argue with myself. I am hurt. Devastated.

"I am trapped with these people for the next five days!" I tell her.

For the next five years. For as long as the Captain sails. I am trapped with Best Buddy and bottles of bourbon, bad jokes, battered boat wives, boozing cockpit sitters, bragging Brits, boring barbecues, barking bearded boat bastards.

Best Buddy is absolutely right. He will outlast me.

The Captain suddenly appears at the stern to take in the colors. He has only a minute to furl the flag before taps.

He barely gives me a glance.

I eye him from the deck. The sympathetic wife backs down into the galley out of the line of fire.

"How could you?" I blow up just before he rushes to rejoin the party onshore. "HOW DARE YOU TELL THAT JOKE TO THOSE PEOPLE?"

"SINCE WHEN DO YOU GET TO BE SENSITIVE WHEN YOU TELL JEWISH JOKES ALL THE TIME!" he shouts back. He looks around, embarrassed at being dressed down in an open cockpit.

"YOU ARE NOT JEWISH!" I yell.

He shouts back, "NO! I AM NOT JEWISH! I CAN NEVER BE JEWISH!"

And the years of squashing cultural rage into my back pocket, years of being dismissed by his Ambassador father as *"that Jewish Woman,"* years of waiting on the side, years of waiting for him to stick up for me, to fight for me, include me, to love me—the years turn into a lifetime of insults. I think he can't see, too worried at what the sailing-club members think of him, to stand by me. And the memories all solidify, become so vivid on their deconstruction that I know it's over between us. I just know it. My eyes see him as a foreigner, a stranger. I can't understand why we are ever together—he is missing such a critical mass of understanding. We are separated by five thousand years of Jewish history. And now he has betrayed me on a boat in the Chesapeake for the benefit of a group of sailors who drink too much, whose wives are rumpled, aging, pink and green and blue and khaki colored with salty brown boat shoes and I cannot breathe, not one minute more.

21:00

He doesn't apologize.

The hurt slaps me down like a rogue wave.

I shut myself in the forepeak. He and Best Buddy and a crew of friends sit drinking in the cockpit, swapping sailing stories until long past midnight. When the last reveler is gone, the Captain opens the bunk door. I pretend to be sleeping, but am hoping he will climb in and say he is sorry so that maybe I can forgive him. Instead, he slips his pillow out from beside me and sleeps in the salon the rest of the night.

7:55 A.M.

By morning it is too late.

Inside the cabin, the temperature reads ninety-nine degrees of heat and climbing. It is not even eight o'clock. I have four more minutes to make the final decision before we push off. When I emerge into the startling sunlight of the cockpit, the push comes to shove when the Captain doesn't look up, or even breathe good morning. Instead, he checks his watch and leaps over to Best Buddy's boat as if on an urgent mission.

There is no good reason to take the heat any longer.

All I can think of is the nearest air-conditioned airport and home.

He leaves me no room, no respect, nowhere to go except out. So I go.

MEAN

BOSTON

I have spent thirteen years in bed with a guy who loves Ernest Hemingway. But I don't think for a moment I write like his favorite author. This book is not literature. I know that. But if it even gets reviewed, I am prepared.

I know what the critics will say; he should retaliate with *Boat Bitch*. But the truth is, no one can say anything meaner than I've already heard, or thought, about myself.

Here's a sample of the Captain's reviews after I jump ship:

You were looking for an excuse.
You have no manners.
My father never liked you.
You move too fast.

I wasted thirteen years with you.
If you really loved me, you wouldn't have walked out.

Let me continue.

Call me:

selfish
impossible
controlling
out of control
demanding
critical
complaining
not one of the boys
unsociable
unreasonable
a toilet-paper abuser
a dry-towel taker
an alcohol-intake watchdog
a waitress pesterer
a restaurant table changer
a hotel-room fault finder
CVS reliant
irritable
impatient
intolerant
intolerable
thoughtless
tactless
clumsy
embarrassing

eccentric
a maverick

Now add these to the list once this book comes out:

an attention seeker
a fight escalator
a kitchen-sink thrower
a secret spiller
desperate

I'm sure there's more and I'm sure he's right.

But there's another side to this story, even if I have to be the one who tells it.

He knows:

I'm a creative cook with bits and pieces of shoelaces.
I tell great bedtime stories.
I'm the ship's eyes.
I read the depth sounder.
I read the guides.
I organize the food.
I make him stop and put his feet up.
I can be enormously charming.
I can be very entertaining.
I wipe his forehead with cold compresses after a hot day in the sun.
I help furl the flags after the ship is undressed.
I hang out the laundry.
I hold the helm in a storm while he reefs the main.
I make him use the autopilot.

I batten down the hatches.

I stow the gear.

I untie the fenders.

I stow the fenders.

I fill the water tank.

I throw the bowline to the gas attendant.

I lug groceries in canvas bags by foot.

I push trolley carts of overweight bags and food down narrow gangplanks.

I get him to swim after a long day looking out to sea.

I point out the dolphins, sea lions, and porpoises.

I hold his hand.

I kiss his neck while he's at the wheel.

I bag and carry.

I step and fetch.

I start the engine (when he asks).

I back her down (when he tells me).

I rev her up (when he shouts from the bow).

I yank the anchor chain into the hold (with rubber gloves).

I hand him the painter (when he rows ashore for ice).

I help him slip on the sail cover at night (he does most of the work).

I take her while he anchors (he's dropping the chain).

I take her when he weighs anchor (he's pulling up the chain).

I take her into the wind while he pulls up the main.

I take her into the wind while he drops the main.

I let the lines out (he pulls them in).

I buy dinner onshore (he buys more).

I make lunch sandwiches (he uses onions).

I cook dinner onboard (he makes linguine and clam sauce).

I chop celery (he does it faster).

I make garbage runs (he carries the heavy bags).

I dry the dishes (he dries them drier).

I use my own money (he pays for all sailing-related costs).

I organize everything.

I scout.

I book hotel rooms.

I make airline reservations.

I change airline reservations.

I share my adventures with him.

I remind him to drink water.

I make love to him.

I find little sea treasures on shore.

I write him love notes and hide them in his pockets.

I buy him books on sailing adventures.

I read to him at night.

I record the wonders of the day in his logbook.

I rub sunscreen lotion on his scalp and neck.

I trim his beard.

I cut his hair.

I file his ripped fingernails.

I care about him.

I worry about him.

I wait for him.

I have a good and generous heart (often hidden).

I love him.

I'm sure every male yacht-club member from Maine to Key West will commiserate with the Captain when this book hits. I know I will be banned from ever using their bathroom facilities again. There will be "Wanted" posters hanging on the club bulletin boards. They will comfort the Captain with free drinks on the house. They will understand exactly why he shows the good sense and breeding to remove himself from such a reckless relationship. The Old Boy Network will take care of him, agree with him, slap him on the back, pour him another drink.

Maybe the Old Girl Network will secretly cheer for me. I think they have very old scores to settle, battle-axes to grind, high seas to climb up on, doldrums to drown in, dry bones to pick. Although they would never ever air their dirty laundry out on deck, they will applaud this book and pass it around under the Captain's table. They will never buy the book, pay actual cash for it, be seen reading it, but they will quote every chapter, and worse.

Later, when the decks clear, both sexes will try to identify the *Who's Who of Sailing*. They will be wrong. And they will be right. It can be anyone.

It just happens to be my someone.

ALONE

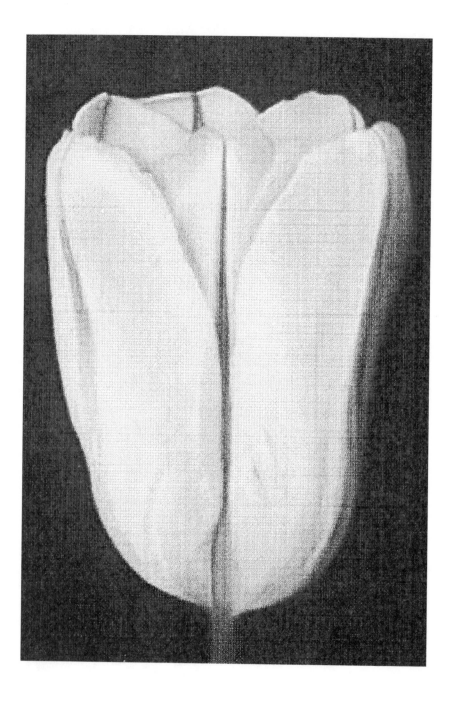

TULIPS

Why do I keep thinking about the tulips?

The final boat escape screws up a lot of previously made plans. For example, we have bought nonrefundable tickets to the south of France to go to a late-June wedding in Mougins. The couple finally getting married is a European version of us. The groom is a handsome, likable, broad-smiled German hotel developer in his late fifties with two previous marriages and children. The third bride-to-be, twenty years his junior, with a black-cat feel and a just-ate-the-bird smile, is an East German Olympian javelin thrower. Already a skilled champion at long-distance shots, she hoists herself to the West two weeks before the Berlin Wall tumbles down and lands in the lap of his luxurious West German hotel. After ten years, one unofficial child, a charmingly resurrected French farmhouse complete with a magazine-worthy herb garden bordered by tall sprays of sachet lavender, the mistress of the manor is finally getting her lover to say *Ich will.*

The Captain and I have not spoken at all in the two weeks since my escape, so when he calls long distance from some watery port the night before the France trip to cancel with a curt *"I'm not going,"* I am not surprised. When he adds, *"And by the way, I'm going to date other women,"* I am surprised, and hurt.

But not crippled.

I go to the wedding by myself.

The next evening I fly off to Nice and find myself sitting next to a handsome young Dutchman, the international sales manager for an enormously successful computer software firm. The next thing I know, we are wrapped up like old lovers. We share our hurts, our family secrets, the stories of our lives; the intimacy of flying and sleeping in such close quarters encouraging the immediate connection. I forget for seven hours who I really am—that I am probably ten years older than he is, that I have a seventeen-year-old daughter, a dog, two cats, a house, a mortgage, studio rent, a forty-eight-year-old body with hot flashes, that I am broken.

Still, the Hollander visits me from time to time when he's in Boston on business. The last time I see him, I ask him if he will bring me some red tulips from Amsterdam. I tell my Dutch friend when they blossom in the spring I will think of him there in my tiny city garden. He promises he will bring me bulbs, but on his next visit, he is empty-handed.

I should have learned never to expect anything a long time ago. But I feel crushed. I only ask for the tulips because my Dutch friend offers to bring me something from Holland. I really want to ask him for a hug, a home, a heart. Something to fill up the hurt. Only I think the tulips are a better bet.

Still, there are surprises. When I am not expecting it, after I recover from the disappointment of his forgetting or whatever the excuse, when I have completely forgotten I have a desire for succulent red Empire tulips that will bring passion into my spring, my Dutch friend comes again on a surprise visit and hands me an export bag of one hundred tulip bulbs; not only reds, but also oranges, pinks, purples, yellows all mixed up, a topsy-turvy garden of colors for me.

I plant them on a late-fall weekend, the very day I know the Captain is leaving for an extended trip to France, this time without me. I plant these one hundred tulip bulbs on my knees, in my postage-stamp city garden. I am not thinking of my new Dutch friend at all. I am thinking of the Captain and remembering ten years back to the garden of my heart, digging 350 six-inch-deep winter beds in concentric circles in the back of the barn, in the back of the house down the Cape, the house I find and the Captain buys to grow old in.

I am remembering how I carefully design a tulip festival of festivals, circle upon circle of red jumbos, parrots, Emperors, French tulips; 350 tulip bulbs by size, by color, by pattern, around and around. Hands blistered, broken fingernails, wet knees, cramps in the thighs, runny nose, aching lower back, around and around until the job is done, the bulbs laid to a winter's rest, the sandy dirt piled back into protective mounds. I am remembering how I think I simply need to just sit back and wait for them to flower.

So I sit back and wait for a spring that never comes—not my spring. Surely the tulips blossom. Only I never enjoy seeing their colors because the Captain's and my relationship expires one month after that November gardening. Breakup #1 comes out of the blue, on a gray day, on New Year's Day, to be exact. I am let go. Pink-slipped by phone. After five years, I am told the girlfriend job is over. *Click.*

Two years later I learn the in-between, herbal-tea-drinking Cambridge ornithologist girlfriend absolutely, positively, has to sow her summer vegetable garden on that same perfect sunny circular spot. Exactly on top of the womb that holds the colors of my visual feast. That her vegetable garden has to be aired, hoed, soil turned, all in the early spring to prepare the earth for the fruits of the summer.

And he lets her erase me.

Not one tulip comes to light my eyes. Even years later, long after the Captain and I find our way back together again, when I remember to go out back behind the barn and see if there still exists even one stubborn little bud, I always return empty-handed.

I think I must be talking about me.

THE SUPPER CLUB

It is my redheaded Israeli cousin who brings it up:

"How many Jews can you fit into a Volkswagen?"

We are stuffing ourselves with turkey and acorn squash and bliss potatoes; the intimate circle we call family now minus the Captain. This includes my two sisters, my brother-in-law, my daughter, my Israeli cousin, his very pregnant Israeli wife, and their tv o-year-old son. My Israeli cousin's very pregnant Israeli wife rolls her eyes—she's heard this joke before. My older sister hasn't, which doesn't mean anything because she never gets punch lines anyway. I watch as she braces her thin frame. Tension mounts. Curiosity, however, gallops.

My Israeli cousin curls his straight man's lip, coughs, and opens his very big, blue, not quite innocent eyes wider in expectation, throwing the audience a naughty redheaded glance I've known since he was a baby in a Tel Aviv crib.

My teenage daughter jumps right in.

"Two in the front, two in the back, and six million in the ashtray!"

Everyone cracks up. We can't help it. We all know it's a terrible, terrible joke, but we bellyache with laughs. Even my British, Anglican Church brother-in-law holds his stomach and tries desperately not to respond. He knows the rules. Jews can tell jokes about Jews. To Jews.

The next one comes like clockwork:

Q: *"Why did Hitler commit suicide?"*

A: *"He got the gas bill."*

Hysterics. Soda water spurts out of mouths, tears run down eyes. I am pretending to be offended, but it's funny. Really funny. My daughter starts revving up. She and her Israeli friends at school thrive on Jewish jokes.

My Israeli cousin again seizes the moment.

"Did you hear about the new Internet site?" (Pause). "It's called *Jewhoo.*"

More roars. More laughs, sobs. It's hilarious.

My older sister stiffens. *"Is this a joke?"* she asks, wondering if she should be appalled.

My Israeli cousin is only too happy to share this discovery and explains the site's address, *www.jewhoo.com,* is the Yahoo on Jews. Jew Outing. It lists anyone famous who has a Jewish parent, grandparent, Jewish ancestry, and includes writers, actors, journalists, scientists, plus page links to anything that has the word *Jew* in it.

My older sister gets professorial. She'll have to tell her class about this, she announces in a teacher tone of voice. She thinks her college students will take offense.

But, in fact, the site is real (I look it up) and it's written by Jews about Jews, and this direct and sometimes overly realistic Jewish version of Yahoo confuses: Jewish headlines, Jewish weather, the latest Jews (Stars of David yellow badge Post-it notes announcing "Jew!" to new additions to the list, same design as "New!").

It's funny. Really. Oh, that reminds me—I should tell my father. He'll love it.

So then, of course, we can laugh at ourselves, only if we laugh among ourselves, and as long as we get there first. Actually, this Thanksgiving is absolutely forgiving—we are all family. With the Captain's place empty, however, only my brother-in-law sits in the non-Jewish seat. He laughs, too.

But he's uncomfortable.

MOONING

HOME, ALONE

Big moon. *Big deal.*

I know it's the solstice. I know it's winter. I have been avoiding the subject of holidays like a Jeep Cherokee driver avoids mountain snow—got all the spanking new equipment but at heart prefers the city. I don't want to get out of my dry bed and back onto the wet boat. Ask me my sign and you won't be surprised to learn I'm a Pisces. Only now I'm a fish out of water.

This astrology-sign business is beside the point. I am wavering. I see I am looking for a way out of what I really have to explain. This festive month practically jumps up from the raw chilly earth like an accidentally stepped-on edge of a metal hoe that bounces back to slap me hard in the face.

I know what's coming. Or not coming.

The Christmas card.

He sends me one.

Funny how I open the mailbox every single day with the caution of a bomb-detector, fingertips inching cautiously forward inside the country, farm-blue-painted mailbox, skirting the piles of holiday sales pitches, department-store promotions, heating and electric bills. I am expecting nothing less than the booby-trap wire to trip and trigger. I know it is just a matter of time, waiting, knowing, expecting.

I am not wrong.

The calls come first from my friends.

Then from my mother.

"We got a Christmas card from the Captain," she tells me, *"No signature."*

He sends unsigned, mailing-list-labeled postcard prints, a studio photo arrangement of messy red-and-green Christmas items in a Mr. Spudbud mug under a plastic evergreen tree. The entire photo is shot against a blotchy red velvet backdrop, reminding you this is a bloodbath of a Christmas card. It is not creative, not anything more than a reminder, a don't-forget-me card, even though he is off in France again.

It is probably his studio assistant's visual. I certainly hope so. It is a mediocre effort, the image, the message. I think I am the only person to understand the significance of Mr. Spudbud, his first big-deal commercial assignment thirty-five years before.

My friends report the card is wordless: no signature, no note. All related recipients are offended. *Better,* my mother says, *not to send anything.*

I do not think I am on Santa's anonymous list. I expect he will dip into my emotional reservoir with one more reminder that is intended to prolong the punishment.

And it comes. The mailman delivereth.

The familiar handwriting, addressed to my daughter and me, scribed in the backhanded, ego-looped letters gives me a start. The handwriting is so immediate; it's as if the Captain himself is lying in wait inside the mailbox. Stamped from North Carolina, clearly mailed by Best Buddy or perhaps his more accommodating wife, the card has a forced cheery Y2K message on the front. No return address, no hint of where in France he is hiding. He is wishing us a truly wonderful year 2000. It is so ridiculous, actually, when he adds a personal note letting me know he will be in France yet another six weeks and is really learning the language.

Forget French, I steam. I just want him to say he's sorry in English.

Now armed with his card, I give the Captain one point for at least having the good sense not to send a Christmas greeting of *Santa Overboard*. There are no watery words, no seafaring hints. Well, except, that is, from where it is mailed—Pamlico Bay, Cape Fear—boatyard territory of Best Buddy, who must have sputtered to port after a loud and opinionated visit to France to shore up his wounded friend. I'm sure the card is mailed against all Best Buddy's natural instincts. But he did it. I think Best Buddy is like the carrier pigeon. Or the rat with Plague.

The truth is I am secretly pleased the Captain doesn't include me in the anonymity of the prelabeled cards, and that Best Buddy has to spring for the thirty-three cents to mail it.

RAIN IN SPAIN

Six months after the Chesapeake debacle, and sometime in mid-January of the new millennium, I run off to Spain for the week alone, on my own, to look at a *castillo* for sale somewhere outside of the Moorish city of Granada. Buying a castle in Spain is a small fantasy ignited by a two-line advert in the International Herald Tribune real-estate section that keeps my attention for several months of E-mail correspondence. The fourteenth-century Moorish fortress is being pushed as a romantic dream castle in "perfect condition" by its secretive aristocratic owners, whom I decide it's finally time to meet in real life.

The Bavarian owner, Baroness-von-Something, turns out to be a sociologist with an extreme obsession with birds. Her also extremely dogmatic, choleric husband, Mr. Baron, is a red-faced, gray-haired, ex-pat type, an exasperated fellow with suspect bloodlines who claims remarkable descent from twelve generations of noble European stock, including King Ferdinand of Spain. He tells me, in an accent curiously American, that his baron father hightails it out of Germany after speaking out a little too loudly against the National Socialist Party in the thirties, about the time the Nazis started making noises about rezoning his fairy-tale family estate. It seems this baron gets the goose-stepping Gestapo boot, obliging him into an ersatz exile in British Malaysia. The baron's son, the present baron of whom I speak, manages to get an architect's education in the States. Mr. Baron then puts his development skills to use by acquiring this crumbling ruin from the Spanish government, which, in the early 1970s, prefers to keep stately but seedy homes in the families of aristocrats. It is either that, turn them into *paradores,* or condo-ize them off for summer retreats to just anybody.

With an infusion of money-talking cash from silent partners, the baron throws on a new roof. Then he adds room-to-room electricity, an underground sprinkling system (to water the naked palm trees), installs four 1970s-style pink-tiled bathrooms imported directly from Middle America, covers the inlaid mosaic floors with gold-and-white sheep-hair shag carpets. And forgets to add a kitchen, because, as the baroness tells me rather shirtily, *who cooks?*

However, if you like upgraded relics, it's quite the find.

The *castillo* sits smack in the center of the main street of a dead-end, dry-boned village that looks as if no one is at home. I don't blame them. I don't want to hang around, either. At first, I think I've made a mistake, or the E-mail j-peg image I use for reference is taken from an angle I just can't place. I park up on the sidewalk, loop my bag strap over my neck, and peek through the electronic grille-gated entrance bordered by wraparound eight-foot-high walls, the color and texture of muddy pink terra-cotta. I am rewarded with a glimpse of a giant, balding palm tree guarding a small stagnant carp pool midway between gate, grounds, and main-courtyard entrance lost in a deep midmorning shadow. There is a sense of a creepy, one-way-only feeling about the place; the no-exit direction of an Arabian harem. The castle is propped up by two round henchmen-looking mini-turrets on either end of the pink main house, which look solidly built to defend against intruders.

I am definitely one.

I stand outside the main gate for a good five minutes before the appointed *castillo* representative acknowledges me. A jean-and-T-shirted young man with a German accent greets me with a hopeful gaze, weak handshake, and slight nod. I am expecting two clicks of the heels, but he is wearing loosely laced boat shoes. Is this a conspiracy? We are 150 kilometers inland, nowhere near the Mediterranean Sea.

After struggling to open the gate with an assortment of massive iron keys, he guides me methodically through the cold, dark bowels of the original structure, down and up secret marble staircases leading to a dozen secluded, even darker rooms fashioned more like mosaic-tiled prison cells. Each bedroom, with its thin slice of exterior light cutting across an intricate labyrinth of Arabesque windows, strikes me as a kind of solitary confinement; a place where masters brick up women behind the walls for eternity; women who think too independently, or are too beautiful, or too demanding. Perhaps if the women are especially lucky, or their crimes not as heinous as mine, they are not erased completely, but kept alive with trays of food slipped through the iron slots in the imposing ivory inlaid wooden doors, the same doors accessed only by the prince of the palace, once every thousand and one nights, for his own pleasure. I specifically notice the great-looking doorknobs.

The guide takes me on through a small servants' pantry, up a few stairs, into the enormous vaulted mosaic tomb of a dining hall. It has potential. However, all I can see is a scene reminiscent of the Indiana Jones dinner at the Maharajah's Palace in the pink city of Jaipur; table service laid for forty-two, shrunken heads in bowls of soup, entertainment by whirling dervishes, and veiled women with diamond-encrusted belly buttons, serving chocolate-covered cockroaches on gold platters for dessert. Even though it is getting on to Spanish high noon, I am hoping I'm not invited to lunch.

In the part of the house my real-estate guide saves for last, I see what is really going on. The truth is, noble title aside, the baron and baroness have an air of not so quiet financial desperation. Along with the *castillo,* I am shocked to learn they also maintain a seventy-five-foot sailboat and feed a personal zoo of at least eighty-five birds of all sizes and sounds that are flying around or are chained to perches everywhere I turn a corner. The shrill screeching of these birds echoes through the cold marble halls, feathers blowing up my nostrils like the airborne white fur of my shedding American Eskimo dog in the middle of August; bird dung, birdseed casings, bird feed is everywhere I step, breathe, sit.

In the private living quarters, which are now bird bedlam,

I meet, eye to beady eye, an albino-feathered cockatiel the size of an anorexic hunting falcon. She is chained to a wooden pedestal, her worn, featherless neck cased in an iron funnel collar. The baroness calls her Lady Di because she pecks at her breast incessantly; self-inflicting bloody holes in her slender bird rib cage. The baroness assures me Lady Di is harmless. Like the "Man in the Iron Mask," she dances sideways on the short leash of a perch inside the gloomy cell of the castle hall, waiting to be recognized as the princess she really is.

I step over pigeons with twisted necks, free-flying parakeets with lime-green feathers, dull sparrows, dozens of birds and mounds of bird dung free-flying throughout the empty, chilly, dark, airless rooms. The baron and baroness's devotion to the birds is so strong, they take all eighty-five of them along when they sail, and keep a hired Third World couple on board just to swab the bird dung off the poop decks.

The fact that they are sailors trying to dump this property in the poorest of Spanish regions to anyone with cash startles me. I see this castle probably requires more maintenance and more money than even a bottomless-pit yacht. Their personalities are too close for comfort. I see them as if I am looking into a tarnished mirror. He is a dominating, know-it-all sailor with a temper to match, and she is the first mate, crew, and voice of reason with one defining characteristic I lack; she knows exactly how to sidestep and tame his outbursts with great finesse, something I never learn to do. But as I examine her bright smile, I don't think she enjoys it one little bit. The sailing, that is. Or living with this bully of a baron.

It's amazing what a title will buy.

But I digress.

I go to Spain to look at a castle for sale. But really, deep down inside where I see more than I want to see, I go to Spain so I can send the Captain a sixtieth-birthday postcard of a bull-fighting matador from Granada with a Spanish postmark.

In short, I go to Spain so I will be away when he turns sixty because it hurts to be at home without him.

THE GREEN SLIPPERS

THE CAPE HOUSE

It takes six months and one sixtieth birthday.

And time.

I forgive him because I still love him.

I finally muster the courage to go down to the Cape house to see the Captain.

I decide to surprise him.

To give him a chance to say he is sorry because I know he is too proud to admit it.

To tell me he misses me.

To tell him that I miss him.

To tell him that he is important.

To hear him say I am important to him.

That he's sorry he chose sailing over me.

That he's sorry he chose Best Buddy over me.

That he's sorry about the joke.

Even though I know he can't admit it.

That he loves me.

That he will fight for me.

To tell him that we must work this out.

That life is not fun without him.

That traveling is not fun without him.

That the dent in the bed mattress is waiting to be filled by him.

That I've been talking to him on paper since I walked off the boat.

That I have turned the blank books into a real book.

To explain to him, to review the relationship.

To make him understand.

Even though I know he is more stubborn than I am.

Even though he's written me off.

Even though he thinks I have lost it.

Even though he said that it's over.

I decide to try again.

He is not expecting me.

At first his face lights up when he sees me at the door. Then he covers his shock by turning furious.

"You can't just waltz back into my life!" He shoos me away from the door with flapping hands. *"Go back to Boston."*

But I don't believe him.

"I'm not going home."

"You can't come inside." He blocks the door. "Not even to use the bathroom."

I use the bathroom anyway.

But I am not expecting what I find; grocery bags of food are on the floor. Enough food for two. An unfamiliar vaporizer is spewing humidity in the living room by the woodstove. The place is a mess of boxes. There are too many pairs of shoes on the hooked rug. The table is loaded with unopened mail. The coat closet is filled with strange-colored jackets.

He is telling me, but I am not listening.

He is telling me the in-between Cambridge ornithologist girlfriend has moved back in, just as a roommate, someone to mind the house while he sails.

I am stunned, but rally.

"If she's just a roommate, why can't I stay and meet her?"

"No," he says.

"Where does she sleep?" I ask.

But I know the answer.

He is nervous I won't go away before she gets back.

I can see her there anyway.

I see her feet imprints under the kitchen table, exactly where she steps out of my boiled-wool green German slippers.

As if she has just left for a minute and will be right back.

As if she has stepped into my slippers for the rest of her life.

"Go away." He brushes me back down the stoop.

"You're a fool," I tell him.

But I know the real fool is me.

I turn my back on him, stumble down the lawn to my car.

I leave the Cape house forever.

But I don't forget.

EPILOGUE

THE LAST WORD

We are better alone together than in public. Less competition. Less face to lose. Fewer people to impress. Less performance anxiety.

He says, *"Watch what I do, not what I say."*

The afternoon before the horrible dinner with the horrible Jewish joke, he says he loves me, that he's glad I am with him.

But I watch what he does.

He jumps over to Best Buddy's boat without kissing me good morning.

He buys the Sunday paper and goes off to read it on a lawn chair under the trees without sharing a section with me, while I sit in the pay-per-load laundry room at the marina waiting for the cycling dryer to finish.

In the rising heat, he walks over to the little marina store to buy extra tonic water for the ice chest and then to the supermarket to buy more bourbon and rum. But he doesn't think to ask me if I need anything before we embark.

He gives me a set of hammered silver earrings and a breathtaking matching choker throat piece the Christmas before our first breakup. I know his second wife turns it down because she will only wear gold.

He gives me an out-of-character exquisite blown-glass perfume bottle for my forty-eighth birthday. The in-between girlfriend is a glassblower hobbyist.

Alone in the Cape house one last Saturday winter's night before sailing season begins, we dance cheek to cheek in the downstairs hallway to the soulful voices of Ella Fitzgerald and Judy Garland. I love him so fiercely my heart hurts. I wish he can zipper me safely inside his chest and never leave me behind. As he holds me close, the small hairs rise on the back of my neck. I feel disaster is coming and tears spring to my eyes. The telephone rings.

Somehow I know this is our last dance together.

Today, nine months after my escape from the Chesapeake, I know he is handing the studio keys over to his assistant, packing up the van, and heading south to sail for the rest of his life.

I know the drive to the boatyard in North Carolina is long.

I know which Comfort Inn he will stop in for the night.

And I know what he is thinking as he drives on the New Jersey Turnpike hardly halfway through the trip.

He is thinking about me.

He is thinking, What a mess.

He is thinking, She walked out.

He is thinking, I miss her.

He is thinking, She couldn't behave in restaurants.

He is thinking, I'm out.

He is thinking, I miss her.

He is thinking, *Why did she have to screw up?*

The Captain

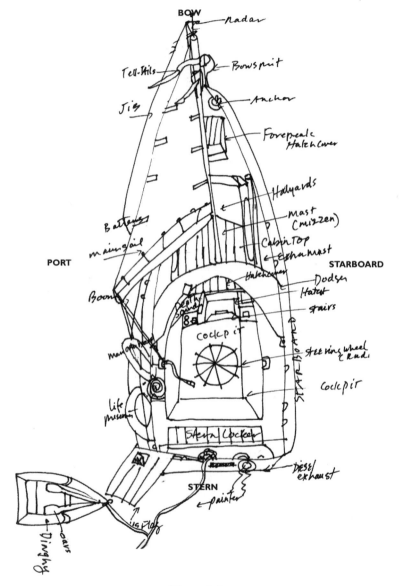

Topsides

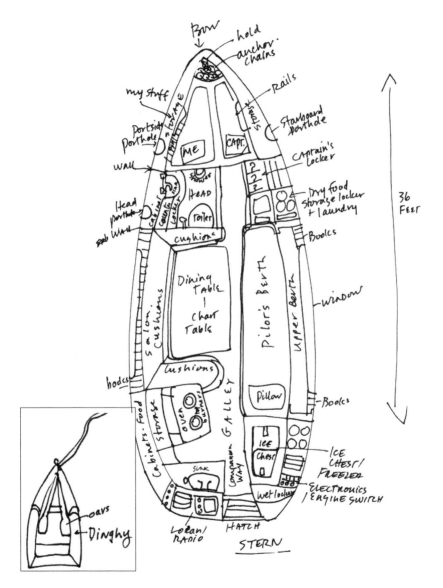

Below Deck

The Boat

"Cockroaches"

"Award Night"

ACKNOWLEDGMENTS

KVR/Daughter & Chief Editor: ("YOU ARE WAY TOO NICE.")

Charles Bell Everitt, Literary Agent: ("Get madder. They're terrible.")

Dominique B.: ("At least benefit from what you dared to do.")

Gale A.: ("I hope you're the main character.")

Felicity: ("He should have married you.")

Annette: ("He should crawl back.")

Stephanie: ("I don't even cut my husband's nails!")

Claudia C.: ("Such incredible neglect.")

Inger R.: ("I never thought it was so bad.")

Margolit: ("Bastards are bigger in Israel.")

Irene: ("Why is he still fighting after all these years?")

Alex: ("The problem is a ship can't have two captains.")

Anne-Mari: ("If it's smaller than a brick, it's love.")

Cosmo: ("I loved you more.")

Trevor: ("As your doctor, I advise you to see a lawyer.")

Chris: ("You are not his priest, lawyer, psychiatrist, even his wife. *What's the moral dilemma?*")

Sue: ("Of course you can be bought. Just make sure there are at least three commas.")

Ansbert G.: ("Send him the manuscript and ask if he has any edits.")

Efrat: ("Think of all the ancillary rights; movie, miniseries, T-shirts, Boat Bastard harbor tours . . . and, by the way, who's designing the book jacket?")

Adi: ("He wanted to ride the bus, but he didn't want to pay the fare.")

Ami: ("It's good my grandma is not alive.")

Tamar: ("Remember, you can have drama with a nice man, too.")

Jasmin: ("He's going to have a heart attack.")

Michelle J.: ("How angry can he get? You've made him famous!")

Claudia K.: ("I hope I have a walk-on role!")

Rozi: ("Give the guy a break.")

Meisa: ("Let him think what he wants.")

Mashaal: ("I don't blame him.")

Olivier: (*"Terroriste!"*)

My Sister Barbara: ("Great title.")

My Sister Joan: ("I hope you realize you'll never get back together after this.")

My Brother-in-Law Peter: (*Twitch.*)

My Mother: ("Why should you be a woman trailing along?")

My Father: ("Don't forget, you also had a lot of good years.")

Jonathan R.: ("I didn't intend to like this book.")

Vivien: ("The book is brilliant. He got away lucky.")

Brian K.: ("I don't know if I want my wife to read this book. She might get ideas!")

Denise M.: ("I love the lists!")

James A.: ("You really need to do something to that Brit who pulled your clothes out of the washer.")

Livy: ("This is totally fantastic!")

Susan G. Everitt: ("If it weren't for me . . . !")

Peter K.: ("I'm waiting for the sequel.")

Andrea: ("Have a book signing party at the Cape House, I'll wear my stilettos.")

Geoff: ("It reads just like you talk. I ran through the whole manuscript over breakfast with a bowl of cornflakes and milk.")

Emmanuel D': ("This book feels like you're being carried away on the tide . . . a tidal wave!")

Lee M.: ("I kept turning the pages standing at the kitchen counter.")

Caroline F.: ("It's all true. I was the baby-sitter!")

Rinat: ("Even I read the whole book!")

Jacob R.: ("Why a bracket?")

DVR: ("He always wanted a book written about him.")

Hal: ("It's very sad.")

FINAL
ACKNOWLEDGMENTS

To the true front line heroes:

Dana Albarella, my smart, "nothing's impossible" senior editor who discovered this project under her massive pile of manuscripts a week before September 11, 2001, said "I want this book no matter what," and kept her word.

Liz Lauricella, her trusty, right-reading sidekick, who read it straight through and announced, "I am this book!"

Dan Taylor, the creative director, who gave me a generous hug after reading the book, and meant it.

And the Farmhouse at Seven Gates Farm, Martha's Vineyard, for restoring me to myself.